JA 8 '68

MIDDLEMARCH
Critical Approaches to the Novel

MIDDLEMARCH
Critical Approaches
to the Novel

MARK SCHORER
W. J. HARVEY
JEROME BEATY
DEREK OLDFIELD
HILDA M. HULME
BARBARA HARDY
J. M. S. TOMPKINS

edited by
BARBARA HARDY

New York
OXFORD UNIVERSITY PRESS
1967

Printed in Great Britain

ACKNOWLEDGMENTS

MY THANKS must go first to all the contributors and then go doubly to the punctual ones, both for their punctuality and their great patience in putting up with the delays that are perhaps less avoidable in a collection of pieces of work in progress than in the ordinary book of commissioned essays.

I am very grateful to Arnold Dewey, of the Athlone Press, not just for his customary care and criticism, but for discussions at a very early stage in which he helped me to see what kind of book this might and might not be.

I am deeply indebted to Gordon S. Haight, not only for his edition of *The George Eliot Letters*, to which all current George Eliot scholarship owes much, but for his personal interest and suggestions.

BARBARA HARDY

CONTENTS

Introduction

I N I N T R O D U C I N G this Anglo-American collection of essays on a great and much-discussed novel, I want to stress its variety first, its unity second. Its variety is not, I hope, too discrete and fragmented. The book originated in some earlier plans of mine for a many-faceted study of *Middlemarch* which were abandoned as it became clear that the kind of work I had in mind would be more efficiently and appropriately written by several hands. Indeed, the book was already being written, by several scholars on both sides of the Atlantic, whose common concern lay not in method or critical dogma, who were attached to no particular school, but who were linked by a close and concentrated interest in *Middlemarch*. The group of complementary and interrelated studies that has emerged is, I think, representative of its time, both in its range and in the way it looks back and ahead in methods and conclusions. The methods and conclusions are of course worked out in the appreciation and exploration of this one novel, but they are also applicable to other novels, past and present.

Most of the contributors were engaged in working on George Eliot and were asked to provide an example of their current research and interests, making of course various necessary adaptations of focus and selection. No high degree of unification was aimed at: I was indeed pursuing the variety of *Middlemarch* through a choice of a variety of methods and interests, though I was especially drawn to work that was close, concrete, self-critical, and tentative. Several of the contributors were already known to each other and were carrying on an informal exchange of views and findings and this meant that the planning of the book was easy and pleasant, though the actual production was necessarily rather slow and the final scope of the symposium has turned out to be slightly narrower than I first intended. Jerome Beaty had been and still is working on George Eliot's texts and manuscripts in preparation for a new edition of her novels; W. J.

1

Harvey had worked on her critics, over a much larger range of novels and reviews than he shows us here, and has also recently become interested in approaches to the 'background' of ideas in criticism; Derek Oldfield had been making a study of the language of the novel for a London University thesis; my own essay was broken off from a study of local effects and surfaces in various novelists. Mark Schorer comes in not simply as a George Eliot specialist but as a critic broadly concerned with questions of imagery, form, and technique in fiction. Hilda Hulme again had worked chiefly on the language of Shakespeare and other earlier dramatists, became interested in George Eliot's imagery, and is present as a most welcome 'visiting linguist', to borrow her own phrase. I suppose J. M. S. Tompkins is also present as a visitor, though her work is of course in the relevant field of eighteenth-century fiction and she has written on other Victorians such as Charlotte Brontë, William Morris and Kipling. She is very aware of her Victorian roots and brings the facts of personal knowledge and memory to our historical reconstruction and evaluations.

It will be plain that the collection represents no school, mixes what we call scholarship and what we call criticism, is specialized in subject and method of work and, as I have already said, looks both backwards and forwards. Some of us may at times seem to run into the danger of fouling our own nest but perhaps this is both healthy and inevitable in a collection of essays written at this time. It mixes formal analysis and doubts about formal analysis; studies of background and studies of foreground; and proffers examples of linguistic criticism of a relaxed and eclectic kind that strike me, as a literary critic usually hoping for more than I get from my linguistic colleagues, as profitable exercises in the combination of literary and linguistic interests. I should have liked to include essays representing historical research and sociological enquiry, and liked still more to have given evaluation and judgment a better showing, but the historians and judges, on this occasion, proved elusive. Historical research of a local and concrete kind is represented here in W. J. Harvey's first essay and there is perhaps something to be said for a critic's scholarship just because it is not quite the same thing as a scholar's scholarship. I think judgment creeps in here and there, even if obliquely. If a poll were held for the greatest English novel there would probably be more votes for *Middlemarch* than for any other work—and not all the votes would be purely pious ones—but it is a novel, like *Madame Bovary* and *Ulysses*, whose stature and status have had to stand up to a fair amount of battering by controversy and attack, and it would be a pity if in this book its flaws went quite unmentioned in the chorus of loud praise.

There is an absence of separate dogmatisms that might have produced violent tension. Contributors do sometimes implicitly criticize each other: W. J. Harvey's illustration of critical reactions to the first version of the end of *Middlemarch* plainly needs to be read side by side with Jerome Beaty's discussion of the revision, but there are few examples of this kind. Tentativeness seems to emerge partly from the nature of the contributions and partly from the time when we are writing. Work in progress, and especially specimens of it extracted and shaped for a collective volume, will almost inevitably move away from certainties towards suggestions, but I doubt if a book like this would have sounded so tentative, say, ten years ago, when formal analysis of fiction was not quite yet in its heyday and when Victorian novels were still criticized for their want of architecture. Mark Schorer was amongst the first critics to analyse the imagery and structure of Jane Austen and George Eliot and he remains more deeply committed to formal analysis than anyone else writing in the volume. But it is relevant to observe that though he speaks in terms of a familiar and much-attacked pattern of criticism when he calls Will Ladislaw 'the sometimes nearly Christlike altruist' it is in terms so qualified as to step outside the old pattern. If more symbol-hunters and theme-staters used 'sometimes' and 'nearly' and 'like' more often, the quarrel about reducing particulars to generalization and character to concept could be given a rest. As it is, this quarrel haunts my own essay and J. M. S. Tompkins's sharp but not intolerant plea for ancient lights. It is an odd accident of critical history that an earlier article of Schorer's is criticized in J. M. S. Tompkins's concluding essay, but it can here be measured against his newest remarks, which seem not only more tentatively phrased but also more fully engaged with the total structure of a novel, with its human units as well as its verbal ones. He seems now to be at least almost as interested in character as in metaphor. I want to come back to this question of character a little later and mention it here as one instance of the gentle erosion worked by time and argument in the structures of the image-analysts. The really maddening examples of structural analysis that still appear are those seemingly written in blissful ignorance of any past controversy, but I suppose it is unlikely that a contributor to a mixed symposium would be in this state of unhampered innocence. One advantage in feeling yourself a prospective member of a mixed bag whose mixture is not utterly unknown is likely to be an increased sense of audience: a sense of neighbourhood will probably stop you making hugely exclusive claims for your darling theory or pet method.

There is of course here the added condition of the specialist's awareness of others at work, some of them his friends and colleagues. A symposium of critics who were less committed to George Eliot and who knew each other's work less well would probably have produced more spectacular clashes and arguments. It can indeed be a pleasure to see how in some collections the left hand has very little idea of what the right is doing and to turn the page from an attack on image-analysis or blinkered symbol-hunting to an instance of the very method under attack, but in this collection such meetings and clashes were never likely. Tentativeness is a prominent feature of the book. W. J. Harvey's questions about the usefulness and relative importance of the facts that he has unearthed are genuine questions, bearing no resemblance to that specious defensive rhetoric most of us fall back on at one time or other when putting a decent public face on the confident enthusiasm of our sense of discovery. Harvey is asking us to answer his questions because we are in some ways in a better position to do so than he is himself. He presents the unobvious facts that were visible to George Eliot as she imagined and wrote out the characters and situations of Casaubon and Lydgate and that are invisible to nearly all readers today. He leaves us to decide how far our response to the novel is changed by seeing what we had not seen before. Harvey's 'for

my part', 'it seems', and 'every reader must decide for himself'
stand beside Schorer's 'sometimes' and 'nearly' and 'like' as
equally refreshing. If the critic is often dogmatic, so, in a quieter
and more insidious way, is the scholar. How often are we (and,
alas, our students) faced by the monolithic assumption that
factual research needs no justification, that facts are solid things,
and that any facts are better than none, especially in times like
our own when critics can flourish like the green bay-tree despite
a rude or rudimentary concern for fact. Harvey's facts arise from
thinking hard about the facts that are inside the novel, and
following their trail outside with a critic's nose, and I think he
wins his detached attitude towards facts by valuing the internal
facts more than the external ones, by having a critic's detachment towards his own scholarship. Jerome Beaty's detachment,
as I see it, works in the reverse direction: he resists the scholar's
temptation to feed the critic in himself who is eager for nourishment, and he avoids the pressure, very vividly present in work
on revision, to seize greedily on his own materials and exaggerate their importance and purposiveness. His materials are less
spectacular than they were in *Middlemarch from Notebook to Novel*
and he does not exaggerate the nature of the facts uncovered but
merely presents their cumulative, contributory, often small and
uncertain interest.

Even negative signs of tentativeness like these are welcome
when we think, as teachers nowadays are bound to think, of the
secondhand, inflated and deadening effect of so much literary
scholarship on the responses and ideas of our students. Opinion
and analysis can be unreal and deadening too, when used as a
substitute for genuine response, but the deadening effects of
criticism may be exposed by a juxtaposition of varying responses
that can send the student back in faith and scepticism to his sole
self. The impressiveness of facts and historical generalizations
is harder to combat. One virtue of a symposium lies in its brevity
and fragmentariness: everything is inclined to be frankly open
and incomplete. It is, after all, only work in progress, and if the
fragmentariness is sometimes irritating it can also work as a
stimulus. Readers who are already on familiar terms with *Middlemarch* will naturally get most from the book, but it could be

useful to students as well as scholars, not just in its indication of certain lines and methods of thinking about this and other novels but in its invitations to continue and complete what is here necessarily unfinished. It would be the extreme of hypocrisy to use this occasion to lament the exhaustiveness of modern criticism, but while admittedly adding to the bulk of criticism with the usual slender excuses I may be forgiven for drawing attention to tentativeness and brevity. W. J. Harvey offers two examples of background study, inviting us overtly to weigh their value and covertly to carry on: at a time when we have whole books on the 'background' of ideas and on the critical reception of an author it is perhaps more than a merely negative virtue to flaunt incompleteness. Derek Oldfield offers us the language of a single character, briefly sketching in some thoughts about others. J. M. S. Tompkins gives a few instances only of gaps and neglected areas. Hilda Hulme combines a long and very close study of some details of imagery with some valuable long-shots in conclusion, again indicating lines to be followed by anyone interested and able to follow. I offer a chapter, not a chapter on chapters. The essays set out to suggest ways of reading and thinking about the novel but do not claim to be telling the whole truth.

The book does not make undue claims for novelty. I do not want to exaggerate its concern with the humanity of *Middlemarch*, for instance, because that would be to suggest that Character had gone out and come back in again, as can truly be said of Shakespeare criticism. One could of course produce examples of work so concerned with structure and symbol as to neglect character but such work would certainly not be typical of George Eliot criticism. We would find better examples of good critics neglecting character in Dickens, say, or in James Joyce, and there is perhaps no need for me to labour the reasons for such a difference. Criticism of a great realistic artist like George Eliot has never really lost touch with character, and would have found it hard to do so. Where character has been neglected it is chiefly in fragmented and isolated articles rather than larger critical studies. It was neglected because structural concerns occasionally elbowed it out but not neglected polemically, as in Shakespeare criticism. It is true that the tendency to treat plays as dramatic poems has had its influences on the criticism of fiction but the mainstream of George Eliot criticism shows a proper concern for character. Much of the work on imagery and structure, if one takes the trouble to examine it closely, is not moving beyond the human interest but taking another way into that human interest. This may be because the novel is a more frankly and fully psychological form than drama, or *can be so*; it may be because George Eliot's concern for character is absolutely central; it may be because the novel, and certainly the Victorian novel, is a less compressed and enigmatic form than drama; it may be because the criticism of fiction, parasitic in many ways upon the criticism of drama, was saved from many excesses and errors by coming after the long revolutions of Shakespeare criticism. There is no concentrated study of Character in this book but nearly all the contributors are aware of the centrality of character. Sometimes it may appear indirectly, without conspicuous advertisement, but it is pervasive and the very unfussed pervasiveness for the most part points to that continuity of concern which I have been discussing. It may be true, as J. M. S. Tompkins suggests, that minor characters have been looked at as functional rather than personal, and it may be true, as W. J. Harvey implies, that modern criticism no longer asks the kinds of question about character that we find in Victorian criticism, but it is not true that character ever went out completely. My own discussion of one chapter makes some suggestions about ways of looking at gesture, movement, sensation and feeling. Derek Oldfield's study of style is fully and clearly a study of character. Even Hilda Hulme's microscopic analysis of imagery keeps its grip on the units of character, and keeps a grip too on the personality and life-language of the novelist.

Much of the analysis is typical of its time in its concern with detail, in its slowness and closeness, and in its assumptions of general purposiveness. One of the obvious interests of including a piece on the reception of the novel by contemporary critics is the sharp contrast provided between present and past, between close reading and coarse reading, between particularized and general discussion, between professionalism and amateurishness, between a criticism introspectively self-conscious and a criticism cheerfully unmethodical and informal. There is a trace of natural guilt and self-reproach in Harvey's discussion. We are all in a useful stage of reaction from our own critical minings, a reaction which may force us to ask, are we as critics exhausted or have we exhausted the novel? In either case are we simply mining low-grade ore? Are the old questions about Lydgate marrying Dorothea and Dorothea's humanist independence of religious belief really the important ones? Was criticism at its best when it was less professional, or when it was professional journalism which had to keep in touch with pre-critical readings rather than professional 'research' competing with the methods and ter-minologies of the Other Culture? It is essential to be warned from time to time of the dangers and sterilities of moving too far away from the reading response to the novel, but it is also plain that Victorian reviewers, especially of serialized fiction, were also liable to move away. It is right to revive and respect the fine technical criticism of Dowden and uncover signs of an implicit recognition of structure and symbolism in others, but we might as well frankly admit that some nineteenth-century criticism, even when passed through a selective net, is superficial and at times obtuse. I can really feel no regret that modern critics have not asked questions like those concerning Bulstrode's unlikely lack of conscience, or Ladislaw's unworthy flirtation with Rosa-mond Vincy: both questions strike me as being asked by insen-sibility about subtlety. There is no doubt in my mind—while lamenting exaggerated preoccupation with structure—where the real superiority in character-analysis lies. We tend to talk healthily—or masochistically—as if our close concern with the text wrenched our attentiveness away from character, but I think this is truer, as we might expect, of the analysis of symbol and themes than of the analysis of imagery and structure. If one is to bring out the structural relations of character, or the pattern of development which makes a temporal pattern, it is indeed neces-sary to look at nuance and detail: if, for instance, we want to point to the parallelism between Mary Garth and Dorothea, a proper study of their formal relations will spring from a sensitive reading of their feelings and conflicts. If anyone doubts this, I suggest as a good exercise a formal analysis of the two crucial scenes where Dorothea watches while Casaubon sleeps and wakes and where Mary Garth keeps her tense vigil over Featherstone. Not only does formal analysis at its most sensitive spring from a sense of character, but it depends on the analysis of details in character in the process of its analysis. Let us not lose our heads in our admiration for the Victorian critics. For one truly moving and valuable piece, like Dowden on the 'second self' of the author, or the historically significant comments on Dorothea's lack of religion, there are many which should strike a modern reader as insensitive and crude when compared with modern psychological analysis of the novels. Consider the discussion that has been carried on by many critics on both sides of the Atlantic, since *The Great Tradition*, about the character of Dorothea, or Maggie Tulliver, or Gwendolen Harleth. This is often a questioning of the assumption of successful externalization, true, but a discussion kept fairly closely to psychological analysis. Discussion which is mainly one of interpretation has loomed just as large: is Maggie a masochist or not? is Casaubon impotent? is Felix Holt lifelike? and Daniel Deronda? is Adam Bede a prig? I have deliberately cast all these questions in brief and crude form but the frankly psychological discussions have been less brief and less crude and have been more frequent, not less, during the last twenty years of formal criticism.

Harvey's most interesting deduction from the comparison of past and present criticism, to my mind, comes when he says that much Victorian criticism was closer to the reading response to the novel. The relationship between response and analysis of response is a vital one and the critic should be aware of the difference between analysing a first response and, say, a seventh. In a review of my book on George Eliot, John Holloway reproached me for distinguishing between a reader's and a critic's reaction to *Romola*, but I still unrepentantly believe that *Romola* is a novel more interesting to analyse than to read and that this difference is connected with its relative failure. *Middlemarch* is a different problem: even while we point out its flaws, we acknowledge its greatness, its depth, its breadth, its broad sweep and constant unpredictable sense of inevitability and surprise, its astonishing feats of what George Eliot called incarnation. We should always try to keep in mind those things that tend most easily to disappear in the analysis of the seventh response: the sense of continuity, the excitements of following the line of feeling, tension and the freshness of particularity. Hilda Hulme asks us to be aware of her possible deflections of this kind, and both she and Oldfield return often to the starting-point in pre-critical response to our first feelings and impressions and ideas.

George Eliot has been called Shakespearean and in looking at ways of approaching her most Shakespearean novel we should perhaps not overlook the ways in which it is like other novels and the ways in which it differs from them. How far can an approach to *Middlemarch* be an approach to fiction? How far does the analysis of the structure, imagery, ideas, characteristic language, individual scenes carry over into the analysis of Dickens, Conrad, James, Joyce? I may seem to be asking the question the wrong way round. Much of the analysis of form in Victorian fiction has come from reading and criticism of the modern novel, where form is not necessarily different but is certainly more conspicuous, where we so often see even on a first reading— sometimes indeed need to see—the resonance of imagery (*To the Lighthouse*) or formal relations of characters (*Ulysses*) or shifts of style (Faulkner). But when we turn back armed with responses which can be forged into tools of criticism we do have to remember the differences. There is little doubt that the relationship between surface and symbol is different in Joyce, different in Henry James, perhaps different in Robert Louis Stevenson, Turgenev and Flaubert. James and Virginia Woolf generally use a highly monolithic style but Dickens is more like George Eliot in his stylistic variation and characterization. I do not want to throw out too many rags of suggestions but only to make the obvious point that where we approach a writer, even within one genre, with hypotheses and questions derived from the criticism of other writers we should expect the questions to be re-formed and at times rejected. Nor do I want to suggest that approaches to *Middlemarch* will help us to make very detailed maps of other novels; but because it is a novel of such range and profundity, because it is a treasure-house of detail and a remarkable whole, because it is a fine and subtle work of art and a creation of character and communities, it raises issues which touch off responses to most novels.

1

The Structure of the Novel
Method, Metaphor and Mind

MARK SCHORER

MIDDLEMARCH presents something of a technical paradox in that here we have a work of widely diffused story materials with very little effort to tie them together by mechanical plot means, and at the same time a novel that creates a powerful effect of unity. Charting this novel, we find five different prominent stories. We can imagine these as five horizontal lines: the first belongs to the Brooke-Casaubon-Ladislaw story; the second to the Vincy-Lydgate story; the third to the Garth-Fred Vincy story; the fourth to Bulstrode; the fifth to Featherstone. The first is a love story; the second and third, love-and-money stories; the last two, money stories. There are certain loose links between these five stories: Ladislaw becomes Lydgate's friend and Dorothea his patroness; Lydgate's wife is Fred Vincy's sister; Bulstrode is related to the Vincys, and, in a more remote way, Featherstone. We can trace a thin and wavering line of relationships over the five stories. But the stories, the immediate problems of each, have no real connections. Now drawing eight vertical lines, to represent the division of the whole into its books, through the five horizontal lines, we see that the Featherstone story ends with the end of Book III, and that the Bulstrode story has hardly begun. But we see, too, that with the death of Featherstone, the least important character in these five stories, the mechanical plot does begin. The book is half-finished when, through Rigg, Raffles is introduced. The intrigue with which the latter part of the book is concerned destroys Bulstrode, of course; but it hardly touches the Garth-Vincy story, it touches the Lydgate-Vincy story only accidentally, it involves

12

METHOD, METAPHOR AND MIND

Ladislaw but in no way alters his condition. The major story interests and the major characters escape this plot almost entirely, and this plot itself develops out of material that is inorganic to the whole. Then how does the book achieve its unity?

The first, and the most obvious, and perhaps the least important way is through the introduction into nearly every book of the novel of one large social scene, where representatives of most of the five stories are allowed to come together. Examples are the dinner party in the first book and the funeral of Featherstone in the fourth. These scenes comprise a kind of external stitching. But there are several kinds of internal stitching that are of much greater importance.

The first of these has to do with the theme of the book as a whole, and the degree to which this pervades the whole. The major characterizations depend on a single value, or perhaps we should say, a single contrast: the quality and kind of social idealism as opposed to self-absorption; the minor characterizations create the stuff on which this idealism must operate, by means of which it must be tested and qualified. We can see the major characters clearly enough on this thematic scale: Casaubon, self-absorption without worthy purpose; Dorothea, disembodied worthiness of purpose; Lydgate, concrete, limited purpose without self-absorption, but his seriousness at the same time excluding too much, for example, sexual attachment and politics; Rosamond, self-absorption without purpose; Ladislaw, like Dorothea, disembodied worthiness of purpose; Mary Garth, purpose in mundane 'duty'; Fred Vincy, self-absorption capable of limited purpose; Bulstrode, self-absorption and distorted purpose. With this thematic scale, George Eliot is able at all times to play a whole range of modulations in contrast and comparison: the contrast, for example, between Casaubon, the anti-social, ostensible scholar in mythology and comparative religion, and his young kinsman, Will Ladislaw, the sometimes nearly Christlike altruist; the 'religious' dedication of Dorothea to the noblest human ends, and the equally 'religious' dedication ('religious veneration' is George Eliot's phrase) of old Garth to agriculture; Lydgate against Fred; Mary against Rosamond; Bulstrode against Farebrother. The interplay is endless, and

13

it demonstrates that if plot is the first actualization of idea in a novel, characterization is the first means of modulating idea, exploring its complexities.

The operation of these two together is the third means toward unity—certain crucial developments, dramatic developments, in which we observe the 'idealism' of individual characters actively enmeshed in what George Eliot calls 'circumstance'—social circumstance. These scenes create the modulations of story, or true plot, that are so much more important than the mechanical plot. They give the book its movement, and it is the movement of the whole that defines the theme. Over and over, George Eliot reminds us of what she calls 'the entanglements of human action', of the complexity of 'circumstance' and the consequent, sometimes excruciating difficulty of the moral life. For the book commits itself to this double proposition: that action is moral, an individual choice that entails individual responsibility; but also, that human life exists in interdependence, that, as Mr Brooke says, 'We're all one family, you know—it's all one cupboard', and the novelist herself: '. . . any one watching keenly the stealthy convergence of human lots, sees a slow preparation of effects from one life to another, which tells like a calculated irony on the indifference or the frozen stare with which we look at our unintroduced neighbour'.

The conflicts between choice and circumstance are laid out in the range of the three major characters. In her marriage, Dorothea Brooke makes a conscious choice out of the fullest operation of which her judgment is then capable; the circumstances into which her choice plunges her, educate her judgment; she lives by the responsibilities of her choice and is freed from circumstance to make another. Will Ladislaw, after choosing to free himself from Casaubon, makes no choices of importance, although his judgment is presumably sound; circumstances never free him to choose, and he finds himself 'on a perilous margin when we begin to look passively at our future selves, and see our own figures led with dull consent into insipid misdoing and shabby achievement . . . he dreaded his own distaste for his spoiled life, which would leave him in motiveless levity'; then circumstances free him at last into a life of choice. Lydgate stands between these two: he chooses consciously, but because his judgment is flaked by 'spots of commonness', he chooses unwisely both in his marriage and in his association with Bulstrode; consequent circumstances force a new and fatal decision upon him, and, with 'distaste for his spoiled life', he drifts into 'motiveless levity'. This 'petty medium of Middlemarch' is the moral universe, and because it is, it binds the book together in a unity not of place but of moral scene.

It is through the great scenes of the book, then, where 'choice' and 'circumstance', or, if you wish, idealism and fact, love and money—where these become 'enmeshed', where the plot gradually closes down on the characters, that the book derives its real movement and life. At the same time, there is a larger, different kind of movement, expressive of the same theme, an opening and closing, *serial* movement, from social idealism to social fact—the breadth of aspiration versus the breadth of the community; a widening scene and tempered values—as in Book I, for example, which starts with Dorothea's sublime hopes and ends with Fred Vincy's hopes of trading a horse. These gradual alterations in view, openings and closings down, each commenting on the other, form the larger pattern of the book. Within these alterations, we must observe at least three different methods of characterization, and observe further how these are played against each other, and what they tell us of the book's deficiencies. (For *Middlemarch* may well be the greatest novel in English, but that does not mean that it is perfect.)

The first group, adequately represented by Mr Brooke and Raffles, are caricatures, the objects of George Eliot's satire, and the most obvious fact about them is that they are incapable of alteration, fixed types. The second group contains Bulstrode, Casaubon, Lydgate, Rosamond, the Garths, Fred Vincy, and others—the objects not of satire but of an ironic sympathy; they are capable of a limited freedom, of some alteration, certainly of self-recognition, and they comprise the great characterizations in the novel. George Eliot's ironic sympathy is evident in her treatment of all of them: in Rosamond's moment of good, for example: in Mrs Bulstrode's great victory over pain; in Lydgate when she writes:

We may handle even extreme opinions with impunity, while our furniture, our dinner-giving, and preference for armorial bearings in our own case, link us indissolubly with the established order. And Lydgate's tendency was not toward extreme opinions: he would like no barefooted doctrines, being particular about his boots: he was not radical in relation to anything but medical reform and the prosecution of discovery. The rest of practical life he walked by hereditary habit; half from that personal pride and unreflecting egoism which I have already called commonness, and half from that *naïveté* which belonged to preoccupation with favourite ideas. (Ch. 36)

This kind of ironic analysis operates just as clearly and as surely in the treatment of Casaubon and of Bulstrode, and in Bulstrode, where the motives are most complex, the method of characterization is most triumphant.

Mr Bulstrode, hoping that the peculiar mixture of joviality and sneering in Raffles's manner was a good deal the effect of drink, had determined to wait till he was quite sober before he spent more words upon him. But he rode home with a terribly lucid vision of the difficulty there would be in arranging any result that could be permanently counted on with this man. It was inevitable that he should wish to get rid of John Raffles, though his reappearance could not be regarded as lying outside the divine plan. The spirit of evil might have sent him to threaten Mr Bulstrode's subversion as an instrument of good; but the threat must have been permitted, and was a chastisement of a new kind. It was an hour of anguish for him very different from the hours in which his struggle had been securely private, and which had ended with a sense that his secret misdeeds were pardoned and his services accepted. These misdeeds, even when committed—had they not been half sanctified by the singleness of his desire to devote himself and all he possessed to the furtherance of the divine scheme? And was he, after all, to become a mere stone of stumbling and a rock of offence? For who would understand the work within him? Who would not, when there was the pretext of casting disgrace upon him, confound his whole life and the truths he had espoused, in one heap of obloquy?

In his closest meditations the life-long habit of Mr Bulstrode's mind clad his most egoistic terrors in doctrinal references to superhuman ends. But even while we are talking and meditating about the earth's orbit and the solar system, what we feel and adjust our movements to is the stable earth and the changing day. And now within all the automatic succession of theoretic phrases—distinct and inmost as the shiver and ache of oncoming fever when we are discussing abstract pain, was the forecast of disgrace in the presence of his neighbours and of his own wife. For the pain, as well as the public estimate of disgrace, depends on the amount of previous profession. To men who only aim at escaping felony, nothing short of the prisoner's dock is disgrace. But Mr Bulstrode had aimed at being an eminent Christian. (Ch. 53)

As he sat there and beheld the enemy of his peace going irrevocably into silence, he felt more at rest than he had done for many months. His conscience was soothed by the enfolding wing of secrecy, which seemed just then like an angel sent down for his relief. He drew out his pocket-book to review various memoranda there as to the arrangements he had projected, and partly carried out, in the prospect of quitting Middlemarch, and considered how far he would let them stand or recall them, now that his absence would be brief. Some economies which he felt desirable might still find a suitable occasion in his temporary withdrawal from management, and he hoped still that Mrs Casaubon would take a large share in the expenses of the hospital. In that way the moments passed, until a change in the stertorous breathing was marked enough to draw his attention wholly to the bed, and forced him to think of the departing life, which had once been subservient to his own—which he had once been glad to find base enough for him to act on as he would. It was his gladness then which impelled him now to be glad that the life was at an end.

And who could say that the death of Raffles had been hastened? Who knew what would have saved him? (Ch. 70)

This is no caricature of hypocrisy; it is an irony that exempts neither the reader nor the human race, and thus it induces finally our compassion rather than our contempt.

It is the irony, one should add, of the finest *mind*. All the more curious, then, the rather gross treatment that is accorded the third group, which is comprised of Dorothea Brooke and Will Ladislaw. As these two escape George Eliot's plot, so they also escape her irony, and almost any passage that concerns them is an illustration of the difference in treatment.

He did not speak, but she replied to some change in his expression. 'I mean, for myself, except that I should like not to have so much more than my share without doing anything for others. But I have a belief of my own, and it comforts me.'

17

'What is that?' said Will, rather jealous of the belief.

'That by desiring what is perfectly good, even when we don't quite know what it is and cannot do what we would, we are part of the divine power against evil—widening the skirts of light and making the struggle with darkness narrower.'

'That is a beautiful mysticism—it is a—'

'Please not to call it by any name', said Dorothea, putting out her hands entreatingly. 'You will say it is Persian, or something else geographical. It is my life. I have found it out, and cannot part with it. I have always been finding out my religion since I was a little girl. I used to pray too much—now I hardly ever pray. I try not to have desires merely for myself, because they may not be good for others, and I have too much already. I only told you, that you might know quite well how my days go at Lowick.' (Ch. 39)

These two, unlike the persons in the first group and like some in the second, grow into awareness, but we can still say, I think, that if the first group is composed of social caricatures, the third is of caricatures of sentiment.

The problem must lie in George Eliot's view of character in general. The general view she gives us constantly: her concept of character is a concept of growth, of alteration, of change, of progress. Character, she says, is 'not cut in marble'; it is 'a process and an unfolding'. One of the means by which character changes we have already observed: the testing pressure of social circumstance on individual choice. Another of the means is in the relation, not of immediate social circumstance, but of public life in general to the private life—'. . . there is no private life which has not been determined by a wider public life'.

Certainly those determining acts of her life were not ideally beautiful. They were the mixed result of young and noble impulse struggling amidst the conditions of an imperfect social state, in which great feelings will often take the aspect of error, and great faith the aspect of illusion. For there is no creature whose inward being is so strong that it is not greatly determined by what lies outside it.[1]

It was no accident, of course, that this novel of social idealism versus self-absorption should have been set in the years when the agitation for the first Reform Bill was coming to its climax.

But there is apparently a third means by which character is

18

formed and by which the individual, in turn, forms the social character. This is in the example of an association with noble spirits. As a novelistic method, it seems to work when Fred Vincy is altered through Farebrother. We accept the possibility when Lydgate just misses the reform of Rosamond. 'We cannot be sure', says George Eliot, 'that any natures, however inflexible or peculiar, will resist this effect from a more massive being than their own. They may be taken by storm and for the moment converted, becoming part of the soul which enwraps them in the ardour of its movements.' We accept it of Rosamond, when the presence of Dorothea galvanizes her into her moment of good: 'it is given to us sometimes even in our every-day life to witness the saving influence of a noble nature, the divine efficacy of rescue that may lie in a self-subduing act of fellowship'. It is, of course, a favourite notion of George Eliot's. She tells us again, 'There are natures in which, if they love us, we are conscious of having a sort of baptism and consecration; they bind us over to rectitude and purity by their pure belief about us, and our sins become that worst kind of sacrilege which tears down the invisible altar of trust. "If you are not good, no one is good—" These little words may give a terrific meaning to responsibility, may hold a vitriolic intensity for remorse.' And there something in the prose, the abstraction, I think, begins to make us feel a little uneasy. It is when the two noble natures come together that our uneasiness turns to discomfort, and the final propositions of the novel seem *not* to have been demonstrated in the *materials* of the novel. For, as Dorothea and Ladislaw presumably fulfil the character potentialities of one another, so, George Eliot tells us in her last paragraph, the things 'that are not so ill with you and me', may be attributed in part to Dorothea Brooke. It would seem to be only here that 'idea'—and the sentimental allegiance attaching to that idea—violates the fine mind (not the noble mind, but the fine mind), and the violation shows constantly in passages where the prose strains to ask us for more response than the facts of the material can justify.

'Drama' and 'discourse' are different and if Dorothea and Ladislaw had been made to operate more actively in the full plot of the novel, this difficulty would have been solved. For the novelist holds the thinker in check. George Eliot the thinker reveals herself in those moments of unattached rhapsody in prose, when the style aspires beyond the objective frame. 'Until that wretched yesterday—except the moment of vexation long ago, in the very same room and in the very same presence—all their vision, all their thought of each other, had been as a world apart, where the sunshine fell on tall white lilies, where no evil lurked, and no other soul entered.' If one can accept as, in some form, an inevitable element in any adequate moral vision, the Pauline confession—'The good that I would, I do not, but the evil which I would not, that I do'—one can see well enough how, in such passages as this, George Eliot's moral vision thins down sometimes to sentiment.

Yet there is a fine mind at work in this novel, and it produces a nearly coherent vision, as well as a unified one. For the fourth means to unity, I should like to look at the language, and more closely.[2] *Middlemarch* is written in a highly explicit metaphorical style, and the metaphors seem to fall into a system that duplicates an established religio-philosophical pattern. (I am, of course, arranging the metaphorical material *in* that pattern.) First: all the metaphors of unification, depending on verbs of mingling, associating, merging, mixing, embracing, comprehending, connecting, allying, binding, making room for, and so on. Second: all the metaphors of antithesis, depending on oppositions between reality and appearance, chaos and order, shapelessness and shape, outer and inner, fact and wish, freedom and restraint, etc. Third: all the metaphors of progressive movement —(a) everyone and everything is 'on a way', and the way can be road, stream, channel, avenue, way itself, journey, voyage, ride, vista, chain, line, course, path, process; (b) with these, we should associate all the metaphors of growth, usually derived from botany; and to these two, we may oppose all the complementary metaphors of hindrance to progress—of labyrinths, winding stairs, yokes, burdens, fetters, etc; parenthetically, one should observe all the metaphors drawn from science, which suggest the special area from which we may expect progress. Fourth: all the metaphors of constructive purpose—(a) of shaping, forming, making, framing, etc.; (b) of pattern or rule, measure or structure; and opposed to these again, the metaphors of the unorganized—Mr Brooke's mind, for example, 'a mass'. Fifth: metaphors suggesting a heavenly goal—of up, high, and higher; of light and fire; of glorious transformation, transfusion, trans-figuration; of veneration, adoration, and worship; of revelation, divination and vision—vision of every kind; of nourishment and fulfilment; of energizing; and finally, of expectation—of 'looking forward'. Let me offer just one example in which all of these seem to come together:

For to Dorothea, after that toy-box history of the world adapted to young ladies which had made the chief part of her education, Mr Casaubon's talk about his great book was full of new vistas; and this sense of revelation, this surprise of a nearer introduction to Stoics and Alexandrians, as people who had ideas not totally unlike her own, kept in abeyance for the time her usual eagerness for a binding theory which could bring her own life and doctrine into strict connection with that amazing past, and give the remotest sources of knowledge some bearing on her actions. That more complete teaching would come— Mr Casaubon would tell her all that: she was looking forward to higher initiation in ideas, as she was looking forward to marriage, and blend-ing her dim conceptions of both. It would be a great mistake to suppose that Dorothea would have cared about any share in Mr Casaubon's learning as mere accomplishment; for though opinion in the neigh-bourhood of Freshitt and Tipton had pronounced her clever, that epithet would not have described her to circles in whose more precise vocabulary cleverness implies mere aptitude for knowing and doing, apart from character. All her eagerness for acquirement lay within that full current of sympathetic motive in which her ideas and impulses were habitually swept along. She did not want to deck herself with knowledge—to wear it loose from the nerves and blood that fed her action; and if she had written a book she must have done it as St Theresa did, under the command of an authority that constrained her conscience. But something she yearned for by which her life might be filled with action at once rational and ardent: and since the time was gone by for guiding visions and spiritual directors, since prayer heightened yearning, but not instruction, what lamp was there but knowledge? Surely learned men kept the only oil; and who more learned than Mr Casaubon? (Ch. 10)

The religious pattern is, of course, the classic account of the mystical progress: first illumination, the vision of unity; return to the world of things, of disunity; dedication to a faith in this special progress of the soul, with a recognition of its impediments; the discipline (constructive purpose) that will assist the progress; and final illumination, the direct revelation of God. But God, of course, is not in this book, or in this system of metaphor; instead, there are endless vistas of unfolding good. And if we shift our perspective a little, we will see that the idea is not religious (although the emotion, in a sense, is) but at least pseudo-philosophical—it is the religion of progress.

I have suggested elsewhere that this metaphorical system serves three functions, expressive, interpretative, and structural. I wish here only to insist that metaphor in *Middlemarch* shows us how thoroughly integrated George Eliot's mind is, and how her entire literary operation is, even in its most intimate details, determined by that integration. The result is, in spite of a loose mechanical plot, a highly integrated novel. I have already suggested how, through character contrast and comparison (Dorothea's religious dedication and Garth's) the many characters are united in a common responsibility to theme. We can go on now and observe certain characteristic actions and comments, which, because the characters share in the metaphorical pattern of the style, are symbolic actions and comments, binding the book still closer. Thus, in the imagery of both purpose and structure, we can see particular significance in Dorothea's concern with planning, indeed with houses; and in the imagery of unification, significance in Casaubon's mistaken 'Key to all Mythologies'; in the imagery of structure, again, Lydgate as a morphologist is significant—'I was early bitten with an interest in structure'. The newspapers, *The Pioneer* and *The Trumpet*, have reference to the imagery of progress on the one hand, and the apocalyptic imagery on the other. Casaubon's trout-stream is a revealing irony on the progress motif: 'Casaubon has got a trout-stream, and does not care about fishing in it himself.' Progress and hindrances to progress both are signified by two statements, near the end, if they are taken together: 'On the road there was a man with a bundle on his back and a woman carrying her baby'; and of Lydgate, 'He had chosen this fragile creature, and had taken the burden of her life upon his arms. He must walk as he could, carrying that burden pitifully.'

It is this style that I should designate as the most effective inner stitching in the novel, for it is this style that, in the minutest detail, externalizes a mind and shows that mind to be one. The metaphorical pattern shows everywhere, but the heaviest metaphorical showers appear, of course, in discursive and reflective passages, either of George Eliot's own or of Dorothea's, and the material as a whole is seen from the point of view of Dorothea's sublimity, temper it as George Eliot finally does. Thus the style of the novel shares intimately in the method of the novel, which allows the author to be everywhere. And thus, tender as the author may feel toward her heroine, the heroine is herself enclosed in the total method, the total vision, and, if only in a *reflected* light, enjoys in some sense the benefits of those ironic evaluations, with their tragic undertones, that are George Eliot's. Dorothea is in this cupboard, along with Mrs Cadwallader and Rosamond Lydgate and Raffles, too. One example of that ironic intelligence that, aspiring as it may up illimitable distances, yet knows the narrowness of human limitation:

In Middlemarch a wife could not long remain ignorant that the town held a bad opinion of her husband. No feminine intimate might carry her friendship so far as to make a plain statement to the wife of the unpleasant fact known or believed about her husband; but when a woman with her thoughts much at leisure got them suddenly employed on something grievously disadvantageous to her neighbours, various moral impulses were called into play which tended to stimulate utterance. Candour was one. To be candid, in Middlemarch phraseology, meant to use a cheerful view of their capacity, their conduct, or their position; and a robust candour never waited to be asked for its opinion. Then, again, there was the love of truth—a wide phrase, but meaning in this relation a lively objection to seeing a wife look happier than her husband's character warranted, or manifest too much satisfaction in her lot: the poor thing should have some hint given her that if she knew the truth she would have less complacency in her bonnet, and in light dishes for a supper party. Stronger than all, there was the regard for a friend's moral improvement, sometimes called her soul, which was likely to be benefited by remarks tending to gloom, uttered with the accompaniment of pensive staring at the furniture and a manner

23

implying that the speaker would not tell what was on her mind, from regard to the feelings of her hearer. On the whole, one might say that an ardent charity was at work setting the virtuous mind to make a neighbour unhappy for her good. (Ch. 74)

That the same mind which makes observations such as this can yet press upon us analyses of the most serious moral dilemmas, shows that it is a mind of range and sweep no less than of coherence and singleness. And one is quite ready to accept—to accept that is, on the evidence of *Middlemarch*, as an aesthetic if not necessarily as a moral or a social fact, this observation: 'The presence of a noble nature, generous in its wishes, ardent in its charity, changes the light for us: we begin to see things again in their larger, quieter masses, and to believe that we too can be seen and judged in the wholeness of our character.' For there is a wholeness in *Middlemarch*, and we see it all in its larger, quieter masses, not in its fragments and its occasional agitations of taste. The material is fused in a moral-philosophical view and is enlarged by a particular method of observation and dramatization. That method has a positive and crucial part in our experience of what we feel to be a work of proportions at once generous and unified; for the proportions no less than the unity are not in the breadth of scene or range of character, finally, but in the mind that views these, and which the metaphorical mode and the method together bring to us with such splendid force.

2

The Intellectual Background
of the Novel

Casaubon and Lydgate

W. J. HARVEY

Scholarship in the humanities, as in the sciences, often seems
to conform to a dialectic in which piecemeal and apparently
random analysis of particular points is followed by the appearance
of a general, synthetic study which aims to chart the whole field.
But no sooner has the map been drawn than the process of
detailed investigation starts again; contours are modified, land-
marks are imperceptibly altered, a new minor tributary is
followed to its source.

So it is with George Eliot. For more than thirty years the
study of her intellectual *milieu* has been fixed and determined
by P. Bourl'honne's *George Eliot: essai de biographie intellectuelle
et morale, 1819–1854.*[1] There have, of course, been a number of
useful essays on particular topics and much valuable work remains
in the form of unpublished theses. But, by and large, Bourl'-
honne's was the full, general book to which one had to return.
This—leaving aside the intrinsic merit of Bourl'honne's study—
has had many disadvantages. It has sometimes been difficult to
assimilate the subsequent accession of knowledge (one thinks of
the great store of primary material in G.S. Haight's edition of
George Eliot's letters). Most writers have accepted the implication contained in the very title of Bourl'honne's book, that

Note. This essay was completed before *A Middlemarch Miscellany* by J. C. Pratt
became available (Princeton University Ph.D. thesis, 1965). This valuable edition
of George Eliot's 1868–71 notebook contains material that extends the argument
of my essay, modifying it in detail but not, I think, contradicting any important
point.

25

George Eliot's intellectual development was complete by the mid-fifties—a very questionable assumption. And, most damagingly, it sometimes follows from this general assumption that George Eliot had worked out a formulated philosophy of life and theory of fiction which she then simply transferred to her creative work. The result of this has been some crude and over-simple equations between the ideas of her novels and the artistic forms which embodied them.

With some honourable exceptions, these assumptions were not challenged by post-war critics, whose main concern was to redefine the nature of George Eliot's artistic powers and to defend her against the charge of being *merely* a disguised philosopher. This led to an emphasis on the formal properties of her work, an emphasis valuable at the time, but one which served to postpone the question of the relation of philosophy to fiction. Clearly this is a complicated question since in one way George Eliot is not an 'intellectual' novelist at all; she never produced a 'novel of ideas' in the sense that, say, *Robert Elsmere* is a novel of ideas. But in most other senses she clearly has the best mind of all English novelists. Hence for some time the question of how ideas *work* in her fiction became more and more urgent until, in 1965, two new synthetic studies appeared which, taken together, may fairly be said to have advanced the problem well beyond the stage reached by Bourl'honne.[2]

Like Bourl'honne's, these are general studies, maps of the whole territory. Some dangers in intellectual history are constant and universal—the temptation, for example, to regard the individual as a kind of Aeolian harp, passively responding to the intellectual breezes of his age, or the temptation to assert too narrow a cause-and-effect relationship between the *milieu* and the person. But there are further dangers in generality; the maps may be too neat or precise to delineate the twists and turns, the labyrinths and metamorphoses of something so protean as the thought of an individual. There is the temptation to tease out into precision and order what is true only when left as part of that confused web of thoughts, emotions, doubts, hopes, attitudes, allegiances and prejudices which makes up a person's total and unique response to life. It is part of George Eliot's greatness that she gives us with so little falsification so much of that total response; it is only in these terms and not in those so useful to the intellectual cartographer that one can finally talk of her 'philosophy'. For all the acuteness, force and rigour of her intellect, George Eliot's outlook is not philosophic in the class-room sense of the word; it is really much closer to the sort of thing ordinary men mean when they talk of having a 'philosophy of life'. As such it is much more tolerant of muddle, contradiction and paradox; it is precisely George Eliot's recognition of this tangle that lends so much conviction to the 'world-view' implicit in her novels.

There is one further complication. Although George Eliot's novels embody a total response she may, for dramatic purposes, allow only a small part of her intellectual range to be represented in a particular work. One has, very often, the feeling that she is working well within the limits of her mind and that what is left, as it were, unwritten in the margin affects that which is there on the printed page. Hence this essay, in which I wish to attempt something that may well seem tedious and irrelevant and which is certainly no more than a footnote to the large, synthetic studies I have already mentioned. It may seem tedious because it involves summarizing information extrinsic to the fiction; it may seem irrelevant because it involves exploring distant and sometimes dingy corridors of intellectual history. Yet the question of relevance is precisely the point of the essay. What light, we must ask, is thrown on *Middlemarch* by the remote, extrinsic and sometimes bizarre information in the margins of George Eliot's creative mind? This is a general problem but *Middlemarch* is a good test-case because it is so ample and well-documented a novel that it might at first seem a fully autonomous work, in the sense that it contains within itself all the information about it that we need to know.

2

I shall concentrate on Lydgate and Casaubon. The contrast between these two men, a contrast which contains many obvious points of similitude, is clearly one of the chief features of the novel's structure. Yet, at first glance, there would seem to be a striking disparity in George Eliot's treatment of them. Most of us, I think, would say that Lydgate is much more fully and carefully documented in terms of his social and intellectual background. His *milieu* is very thoroughly explored and his intellectual interests expounded in some detail. Casaubon's social position is taken for granted and his intellectual interests, though insistently referred to, figure in the novel as no more than a matter of hint and allusion, of casual mention of Lowth or Warburton or Bryant.

Why should this be so? One general answer might be that George Eliot realized that if she documented Casaubon in the same detail as Lydgate the novel would be overburdened with a mass of exposition difficult to assimilate to the narrative flow. This is true but it only pushes the problem back one stage so that we must now ask why she favours Lydgate and not Casaubon or why she does not take the background to *both* characters equally for granted. If we look at the evidence of her letters and journals or of the Quarry for *Middlemarch* we find that George Eliot did a great deal of research necessary to the creation of Lydgate—writing to doctors, reading back-files of the *Lancet* and so on—whereas she did little for Casaubon. Yet this proves nothing since, as we shall see, George Eliot was so familiar with the body of intellectual interests figured by Casaubon that she had no *need* to do fresh research; had she wished she could have documented him out of thirty years' experience of the life he represents. Of course, Casaubon's social position was so familiar, not only to George Eliot but also to her audience, as not to need documentation. The Anglican cleric, in all his doctrinal variety, was an extremely common figure in fiction. But this is not true of Casaubon's peculiar intellectual interests. Moreover, the doctor was also a familiar fictional figure—thus we must ask what was so novel about Lydgate as to demand fuller documentation?[3]

Here we must note one important difference between the two characters. Casaubon's intellectual life has nothing at all to do with either his religious life—which is even more non-existent than Mr Cadwallader's—or with his position in society. It is this divorce between the different aspects of the man that gives a particular ironic weight to the futility of Dorothea's 'eagerness for a binding theory which could bring her own life and doctrine into strict connection with that amazing past, and give the remotest sources of knowledge some bearing on her actions' (Ch. 10) or—and here the irony is heavier—her idea that 'perhaps even Hebrew might be necessary—at least the alphabet and a few roots—in order to arrive at the core of things, and judge soundly on the social duties of the Christian' (Ch. 7).

In strong contrast we are told that Lydgate 'carried to his studies in London, Edinburgh and Paris, the conviction that the medical profession as it might be was the finest in the world; presenting the most perfect interchange between science and art; offering the most direct alliance between intellectual conquest and the social good' (Ch. 15).

Between 'the social good' and the 'intellectual conquest', between his medical practice and his private researches, there is initially no divorce for Lydgate. They are tragically sundered by his marriage. And, because initial connection and subsequent divorce needs more demonstration than simple divorce, George Eliot must treat Lydgate in greater detail than Casaubon.

In one of his essays John Stuart Mill commented that: 'In every religious record handed down from remote ages there is always much which, to advanced culture, seems inappropriate or false; but men do not pass suddenly from one system of thought to another; they first exhaust every imaginable expedient for reconciling the two.'[4] While Mill's remark is appropriate to Casaubon's age it is not appropriate to Casaubon himself. This is indeed perhaps the main point to be grasped about his scholarship; that it is in no sense an expedient for reconciling a system of thought to religious belief—as I have said Casaubon exhibits *no* religious life in any real sense of the phrase; indeed his researches are an escape route rather than an exploration, an attempt to disguise from others and even from himself the sense of human failure, the cold vacuum at the core of his being. Moreover, as the novel insists, his labours are misdirected, anachronistic and futile. To see why this is so we must explore his intellectual context and unravel two strands which cross and tangle in the late eighteenth and early nineteenth centuries—the development of the Higher Criticism and the interest in Mythography. If in following these clues, I seem to turn into a Casaubon myself, I apologize; the subject has a certain mouldering fascination and, if labyrinthine, does eventually lead back to the novel.

Let us dispose first of the Higher Criticism. I have already said that George Eliot had no need to do special research on this aspect of intellectual background; so familiar was she with the subject that she could in a sense have echoed Flaubert—'Casaubon, c'est moi'. Of course, Hennell's *Inquiry concerning the Origin of Christianity* had played a crucial part in her own development, but I think the two primary documents for our purpose are her review of R. W. Mackay's *The Progress of the Intellect* in the *Westminster Review* (January 1851) and her translation, some years earlier, of Strauss's *Das Leben Jesu*. I shall lean heavily on the latter for my account of the Higher Criticism since we can thus be sure we are dealing with material George Eliot knew by heart.

Strauss begins with the same point as Mill, with the clash between ancient or sacred records taken literally and interpretations put upon them by more intellectually sophisticated ages. This is especially true of allegedly divine records which purport to tell of 'the immediate intervention of the divine in human affairs', since intellectual progress 'consists mainly in the gradual recognition of a chain of causes and effects connecting natural phenomena with each other', so that the rational mind will come to see ancient records only as 'mediate links' and not as the literal word of God.

Given this clash, Strauss postulates two possible reactions: (1) The divine cannot have happened as recorded; (2) The records are true but that which has so happened cannot have been divine.

That being so men will adopt one of two methods of resolving the clash: (1) They will find allegorical meanings in the records, e.g. the Gods will represent forces of nature or will have some ethical signification; (2) They will take the records as history but will see them as the records of ancient men, not of gods.

Strauss points out that the Greeks reacted in both ways to the writings of Hesiod and Homer and he finds the same thing happening very early in the interpretation of Hebrew records. Thus Philo, when the story seems unworthy of God, when it is overtly anthropomorphic or self-contradictory, takes refuge in allegory. Thus Origen recognizes the divine in the records but denies it actually manifested itself in so immediate a manner. The modern representative of this reaction for Strauss is Kant, who sees divine records as allegories of the ethical ideas and imperatives which interested him. One offshoot of the reaction towards allegory which was later developed by German critics was the doctrine of Accommodation; this is the idea that writers of divine records accommodate their meaning to the limitations of their audience; when this audience is ignorant or barbarous the result may seem unedifying or untrue to later ages. As one German theologian, Semler, puts it: 'Do not the better informed often find it expedient, when dealing with ignorant persons, to adopt their ideas and language; and do not priests habitually resort to the arts of the rhetorician?'

So much for the allegorical approach. The other mode of interpretation acknowledges the events recorded to be histori- cally true but assigns them to a human and not to a divine origin; this naturally is the line taken in early days by heretics or by enemies of Christianity; it recurs again with some of the deists and free-thinkers of the eighteenth century—Toland, Boling- broke, Wollaston—who apply it not merely to the Old Testa- ment but also to the miracles of Jesus. It develops also in eighteenth-century Germany; for example in the so called Wolfenbuttel fragments published by Lessing in 1774, in which divine communication is attacked as mere pretence and miracles dismissed as illusions, 'practised with the design of giving stability and efficiency' to Hebrew laws and institutions.

A mild proponent of this view might allow that the Deities of popular worship were probably once good and benevolent people who were later deified by posterity; a hostile proponent, on the other hand, would argue that divine records stem from artful imposters and cruel tyrants who 'had veiled themselves in a nimbus of divinity for the purpose of subjugating the people to their dominion'. It is this kind of approach George Eliot deplores in her review of Mackay:

The introduction of a truly philosophic spirit into the study of mythology—an introduction for which we are chiefly indebted to the Germans—is a great step in advance of the superficial Lucian-like tone of ridicule adopted by many writers of the eighteenth century.

As George Eliot notes, those German scholars who lay the foundations of the Higher Criticism—Eichhorn, Paulus, Baur and Strauss himself—while anxious to find natural origins for divine records are also concerned to stress that the processes involved are morally blameless. Eichhorn's great contribution is to stress that Hebrew history must be treated in the same way as pagan history; the records are due to the different phraseology and habits of mind of a primitive age which we must now translate into our own idiom.

The deistic idea of imposture could only occur to those refusing to interpret ancient records in the spirit of their age. Had those records been composed at this day, we should certainly be driven to the alternative of miracle or intentional deceit; but the fact is otherwise; we have here the produce of simple uncritical minds unreservedly using their own conceptions and phraseology.

This growth of the historical sport of interpretation—with its study, for example, of the processes of oral transmission—leads to a view of divine records as myths, as the natural process of time and change.[5] The study of religion is assimilated to the study of mythology in general. Whereas the Renaissance treatment of mythology was concerned primarily with the adjusting of pagan fables to the Christian faith, this process is now reversed; the structure of both Old and New Testament are seen as examples of mythical structure and the groundwork is laid for a comparative study of religion.

Where does Casaubon's attempt to find the key to all Mythologies fit into this? It has often been assumed that when Ladislaw in Chapter 21 tells Dorothea that 'If Mr Casaubon read German he would save himself a great deal of trouble' he is referring to those pioneers of the Higher Criticism I have already mentioned. (It should be noticed that if this were the case Mr Casaubon's ignorance was shared by practically all his fellow Anglicans.)⁶ But it is not precisely so. Casaubon's efforts must, alas, be referred to a much less dignified context.

When an intellectual upheaval such as the one I have described takes place it is a long and confused process and often throws up many lunatic by-products. One such by-product of the attempt to treat Christianity in a philosophical and historical manner was the pseudo-science of mythography, which has indeed, deep roots, but which flourished in the late eighteenth and early nineteenth centuries. This is the dingy niche in which Casaubon, I fear, must be placed.⁷

Eighteenth-century mythography begins by opposing the prevailing tendency to reduce the Bible to myth and, in a sense, continues the Renaissance approach. But whereas the Renaissance generally reconciles pagan fable to Christianity by allegory the mythographer starts by trying to explain pagan myth as a corruption of facts recorded in the Bible; in other words he, too, uses an historical method though one which, as we shall see, needed an unusually large dose of ingenuity and imagination. There are later and more fantastic developments of mythography; one relatively sane approach was to find a rational basis for myth by seeing it as the embodiment of natural forces; another saw myth as symbolic particularly of the procreative powers. This led in the early nineteenth century to a flood of phallic symbol hunting, of the most comprehensive, ingenious, hair-raising kind. But it is mainly with the historical mythographer that we are concerned. George Eliot in her review of Mackay notes that the Higher Criticism is superior not only to eighteenth-century rationalism but also to 'the orthodox prepossessions of writers such as Bryant, who saw in the Greek legends simply misrepresentations of the authentic history given in the book of Genesis'.

Casaubon, of course, is characterized by Ladislaw as 'crawling a little way after men of the last century—men like Bryant'. But Jacob Bryant, whose *A New System, or an Analysis of Ancient Mythology* (1774–6) was amazingly popular, was relatively late in the traditions of historical mythography.

All the mythographers, like Casaubon, were seeking for a single key. Faced with a great diversity of race, custom, creed and fable they attempt to trace all these back to a single origin and square events and myths with the Bible. The single original culture is the world before the Flood; and the process of corruption and diversification is seen as a result of the scattering of peoples after the destruction of the tower of Babel.

I will not attempt to describe in detail the extreme fringes of what is in itself a lunatic fringe; such speculations involve a great deal about the Druids—the Celts are a favourite candidate for one of the lost tribes of Israel—and about the sunken city of Atlantis. This mish-mash is not unimportant—some of it filters down into Mormonism, for example—but even Casaubon does not go to such extremes.

Rather, like Jacob Bryant, he would be concerned to reduce all myths into variants of the Bible story. Like Bryant he would have been plastic in adjusting inconvenient chronologies and like Bryant he would have supposed a single original language which was lost with the Tower of Babel. This concern with philology is important; George Eliot herself tells us that Casaubon's theories 'floated among flexible conjectures no more solid than those etymologies which seemed strong because of likeness in sound, until it was shown that likeness in sound made them impossible'.

This is indeed true of the mythographers—the attempt to trace every word back to a supposed Hebrew root which was diversified by the Tower of Babel led to a great deal of etymological confusion. Light began to dawn at the end of the eighteenth century when Sir William Jones founded the Asiatic Society in 1784 and suggested that Sanskrit might be the common link between European languages. In 1816 a German scholar, Franz Bopp, elaborated the idea of an Indo-European family of languages, and in 1819 Jacob Grimm demonstrated the linguistic connections of diverse languages.

Thus when in Chapter 22 Ladislaw points out that Casaubon, unlike the German, 'is not an Orientalist', he is merely underlining the backwardness and futility of Casaubon's scholarship. Casaubon's whole attempt—though he does not know it because he cannot read German—has been exploded in 1825 by the publication of Otfried Muller's *Prolegomena to a Scientific Mythology*, a work referred to by George Eliot in her review of

Mackay. Muller ruled out all so called etymological proofs that tried to relate diverse myths to a Hebrew origin and showed conclusively that mythologies developed independently; there was no chance of resolving the Many into the One. Thus Casaubon, through ignorance, is a complete anachronism, lost in the labyrinth of an exploded pseudo-science. What George Eliot explicitly says in the novel is fully confirmed by plumbing the intellectual history which lies beyond or beneath her fiction.

I shall not attempt to deal with the context of Lydgate's researches at such tedious length. Though George Eliot did a great deal of research on Lydgate's background she would, through G. H. Lewes, have met at first hand most of the men and ideas who go to form this historical context.

It has often been pointed out that the intellectual aspirations of Casaubon and Lydgate run parallel—both of them are seeking for a key, both of them are trying to resolve diversity and plurality into a basic unity. It is agreed that whereas Casaubon's activities are futile Lydgate's are noble, and it is commonly assumed that his life illustrated the blighting effects of his marriage on intellectual hopes that would otherwise have been fulfilled. But this last assumption is not strictly true; we know that George Eliot was generally suspicious of anything in the nature of *a* key to the meaning of life and in fact she carries the parallel between Casaubon and Lydgate a stage further by insisting that *both* of them are fundamentally mistaken in the nature of their research. The evidence is obvious with Casaubon but with Lydgate it resides in one brief remark which tends, I think, to get overlooked. The passage occurs in Chapter 15 in which George Eliot discusses Lydgate in relation to the great French physiologist, Bichat.

This great seer did not go beyond the consideration of the tissues as ultimate facts in the living organism, marking the limit of anatomical analysis; but it was open to another mind to say, have not these structures some common basis from which they have all started, as your sarsnet, gauze, net, satin and velvet from the raw cocoon? . . . What was the primitive tissue? In that way Lydgate put the question— not quite in the way required by the awaiting answer; but such missing of the right word befalls many seekers.

The comment is light because George Eliot does not wish us to think of Lydgate's endeavours as futile in the same way as Casaubon's. Indeed, they are not futile; for as T. H. Huxley said in an essay on cell-theory on which George Eliot made notes in the *Middlemarch* Quarry: 'There are periods in the history of every science when a false hypothesis is not only better than none at all, but is a necessary forerunner of, and preparation for, the true one.' This comment places Lydgate; it is in this sense that George Eliot can make it quite clear, without detracting from him, that he was mistaken in the direction of his research.

The problem then is—how precisely can we define Lydgate's mistake? One possible answer is in philosophical terms—that Lydgate may, in Huxley's terms, be confusing the familiar 'Matter' with a real entity. Both Huxley in 'The Physical Basis of Life' (an essay remarkably close in so many ways to George Eliot's own outlook) and Lewes in *Problems of Life and Mind* dilate on this fallacy.

But I suspect that George Eliot is thinking here in more specifically biological terms—that what is missing from Lydgate's question is any reference to cell-theory. Without going into the history of nineteenth-century biological thought I think we can say this is the right answer because it functions in terms of the novel itself.[8] In this way while the irony of Casaubon is that he is in ignorance of the real work already done by German scholars in the near-past, the irony of Lydgate is that he is just too soon for the real work to be done, again by German scholars, in the near future. This gives a particular emphasis to 'the awaiting answer'. Casaubon's mistake is his own fault, Lydgate's mistake is an accident of history. In his day his microscope would not have been good enough for the work to be done; Robert Brown—mentioned elsewhere by Lydgate—only did his vital work on the cell nucleus in 1831; the crucial break-through by the German biologists, Schwann and Scheider, was to come a few years later in 1838–9. By that time Lydgate had dwindled to a fashionable practice and a treatise on Gout. Poor Lydgate—his research, like his medical practice, is just a little too premature. And there is, incidentally, one final irony, disconnected with the novel, that George Eliot was herself limited in her biological knowledge, that biochemistry has, after all, brought us back from cell-theory as she knew it to something like Lydgate's notion of primitive tissue.

3

One function of this essay has been to show that George Eliot's mind is like the National Gallery; for every canvas on display there are two stored away in the basement. Granted that the full range of her mind does not always display itself in her fiction the question of relevance reasserts itself. This is something every reader must decide for himself. For my part, whereas the documentation of Lydgate's status as a practising doctor is vital, since it affects the social pressures which circumvent him, the delineation of his and Casaubon's purely intellectual *milieux* is relatively marginal. Nevertheless, it seems to me to brace and support the novel while remaining largely invisible; the comforting sense of amplitude, solidity or density that we derive from the actual novel is thereby reinforced. Moreover, it does put Lydgate's research aspirations in a slightly different perspective and it does help to define more precisely those overlapping areas of similitude and difference which he shares with Casaubon, so that we can adapt to these two characters what Henry James once said of Lydgate and Dorothea: 'The mind passes from one to the other with that supreme sense of the vastness and variety of human life, under aspects apparently similar, which it belongs only to the greatest novels to produce.'[9]

3

The Text of the Novel

A Study of the Proof

JEROME BEATY

THE apparently authoritative obituary article in *Blackwood's Magazine* for February, 1881, claimed that George Eliot 'had rarely much to correct in her proof-sheets',[1] yet there are nearly eight hundred differences, excluding punctuation, between the manuscript version of *Middlemarch* and the best text of that novel, the Cheap Edition of 1874. At most, one hundred of the variants can be attributed to printers' errors and other accidental or mechanical matters. George Eliot herself, or she and George Henry Lewes, made at least five hundred corrections or revisions in the proof of the first edition (published in half-volume parts, December 1871 to December 1872). She—or they—made about one hundred further changes in reading proof for the 1874 edition.[2] Most of these revisions, of course, are relatively trivial, scarcely changing the shape and nature of the novel, and these can best be presented in a critical edition. Patterns of changes and lengthy or significant changes, however, deserve independent presentation and individual discussion, which a critical edition does not afford. It is to these that this essay will chiefly devote itself.

A few of the changes made in the text of *Middlemarch* subsequent to the completion of the manuscript have been previously noted. Gordon S. Haight's Riverside Edition of the novel (Boston, 1956) indicates about twenty, most of them relatively minor—e.g., the changing of character names from Shaw to Standish and from Dove to Garth,[3] the locating of Lydgate's family in Northumberland rather than in Somersetshire, the eliminating of an anachronistic reference to 'Lays of Ancient

Rome'. Two of the changes Haight notes are extensive and significant. The first deals with the scene in Chapter 24 in which Fred comes to the Garths to confess that he cannot pay a debt for which Mr Garth co-signed. In the manuscript version he finds Mr and Mrs Garth together, but several pages were added in the proof of the first edition to show Fred initially encountering Mrs Garth, who had not known of her husband's commitment, and only later confronting Mr Garth. The second indicates that the next to last paragraph of the 'Finale' was significantly reworded for the 1874 edition. *'Middlemarch' from Notebook to Novel* notes two or three minor proof changes and one significant change, the renumbering of the last chapters of Book II and the first chapters of Book III reversing the order of the chapters dealing with Fred's failure to meet his debt and those dealing with Dorothea in Rome.[4]

There are thus well over seven hundred variants, most of them author's changes, between the completed manuscript and the 1874 edition, which have not been noted. The balance of this essay will deal with approximately one hundred of these.

The first fifty may be disposed of rather quickly. They are individually very minor but have some cumulative interest, if not importance, in that they fall into five distinguishable categories: the elimination of contractions, the representation of dialect, the Englishing of foreign words or phrases, the attribution of literary allusions or quotations, and the change of fictional names.

A minor concern, but one that vexed George Eliot both in writing and revising at least from the time of *Adam Bede*, is that of the use of contractions in dialogue. While on occasion phrases that are spelled out in manuscript are contracted in proof (there are two such in *Middlemarch*[5]), in the vast majority of such adjustments contractions in the manuscript are spelled out in revised proof. There are about twenty such changes in the proof of *Middlemarch*, almost all of them deliberate changes by the author rather than printers' liberties with the manuscript. All of them occur in dialogue; the speakers are: Plymdale, Featherstone, Mr Brooke, Will and Bulstrode once each; Lydgate twice; Dorothea three times; Caleb four times; Fred seven times.

These spellings out are about equally divided between the verb-negative forms ('can't', 'mustn't', 'doesn't', 'couldn't') and the pronoun-verb forms ('I'm', 'we've', 'you'll', 'it's'). The strongest indication of the direction of such changes seems to be the number relating to Fred and the fact that all of these appear in the final third of the novel. The issue would seem to be not so much that of accurately representing spoken language as that of suggesting social, intellectual and even moral status. Though an occasional contraction even in the speech of a Dorothea seems not only necessary but desirable—to distinguish her from the pedantic Casaubon, for example—there are many indications that the slangy Fred, sent down from university, reprimanded by his socially pretentious sister, in discovering himself by rejecting the socially acceptable ministry and going to work for Mr Garth, elevates his language proportionally to his proper moral choice and inversely to his social status.

The spelling out of four contractions in the speech of Caleb Garth, who has so much smaller a part in the novel than does Fred, suggests a similar effort to dignify his role or solidify his position as a moral norm. This is reinforced by the spelling out in proof revision of ''em' and ''emselves'(Ch. 56),[6] which changes are closely related to the spelling out of contractions.

The other changes involving representations of spoken language are more ambiguous. Two involve the illegibility of the manuscript. In a bit of Featherstone dialogue 'spirited' appears to be overwritten as 'spirity' (Ch. 12), but the standard form is set in type and allowed to stand; Hiram, one of the farm workers who tries to prevent Garth's surveying for the railway, says 'was' in proof which George Eliot changes to 'war' (Ch. 56), though whether the word ends in manuscript with 'r' or 's' is difficult to determine. In the proof of the first edition she also revises 'of' to 'o'' in a line spoken by the barber, Mr Dill (Ch. 71). Solomon Featherstone's 'forrard' she revises to 'for'ard', which seems largely a mechanical matter. Two other dialect spellings—'fortin' and 'recken' (Ch. 14), both Peter Featherstone's—were apparently normalized by printers in setting the first edition and left to stand, and a third dialect spelling changed—'hive' to 'hev' (Ch. 39)—either by the

printer or author (there is no corrected proof of the first edition
for this passage).

The next two groups of minor changes—the Englishing of
foreign words and phrases and the attribution of literary
allusions—appear quite different in intent from those dealing
with dialogue. Here the concern seems to be to adjust the habitual frame of reference of the intellectual, cosmopolitan author
to that of the popular audience, at any rate in matters of relatively little importance.

At least three French words or phrases were changed in favour
of English equivalents in the proof of the first edition: *'juste
milieu'* becomes 'balancing point'—after having first been
changed to 'safe mean'—(Ch. 32); *'foison'* becomes 'food' (Ch.
48) and *'naïve'* becomes 'ingenuous' (Ch. 61). There is no reason
to believe that three similar changes, made in Book IV for which
corrected proof does not survive, are not those of the author:
'chiffons' to 'clothes', *'dot'* to 'dowry' and *'à propos* of the
wedding journey' to 'when the wedding journey was being
discussed' (Ch. 36). Another foreign term is eliminated between
manuscript and first edition with no evidence of the author
having had a part in the change (indeed the term missing from
the first edition had been set in type and appears in the author's
copy of the proof: 'of *prima facie* misjudgments' appears in the
first edition simply as 'of misjudgments' (Ch. 45). Still another
change was made in the 1874 edition, 'her *fiancé*' becomes 'her
lover' (Ch. 15); though the author did not make the change, she
let it stand in proof.[7]

For some inexplicable reason the attribution of the motto to
Chapter 65 was made more explicit in proof of the first edition:
'Canterbury Tales' becomes 'Chaucer: *Canterbury Tales*'. (One
would be tempted to infer that this further identification was
merely an attempt to make attributions parallel, but such is
clearly not the case: the motto to Chapter 61, for example, is still
identified merely by *'Rasselas'*.) Two lines of poetry in the text
—'"Queens hereafter might be glad to live Upon the alms of her
superfluous praise"' (Ch. 47)—are introduced by the addition of
a passage in proof: 'he might have boasted after the example of
old Drayton, that . . .'. In 1874 proof still another identification

is made: 'Will had a "passionate prodigality" of statement' is expanded to 'Will had—to use Sir Thomas Browne's phrase—a "passionate prodigality" of statement' (Ch. 37).[8] There is a vague, hypothetical 'attribution' inserted in the passage that reads in manuscript: 'Becoming a dean or even a bishop would make little difference, I fear, to Mr Casaubon's uneasiness. Behind the big mask and the speaking-trumpet, there must always be our poor little eyes. . . .' The second sentence now begins, 'Doubtless some ancient Greek has observed that behind . . . ' (Ch. 29). The vagueness of the attribution suggests that this is not an attempt to imitate Mr Casaubon's scholarly style, though some mockery may be implied, Casaubon being more likely to accept a psychological generalization attributed to an ancient Greek than one from the voice of the author; in any case, the *ex cathedra* tone of the pronouncement is somewhat lessened by the interpolation.

George Eliot frequently tinkered with fictional names. The two proof corrections of names Haight indicates were oversights, one or more appearances of an original name having slipped into proof after the name had been changed elsewhere in the manuscript. There are other changes of names in proof. Mrs Carter, Brooke's cook or housekeeper, is three times on the same page called 'Mrs Tucker' until proof was revised (Ch. 6).[9] Mrs Cadwallader's Christian name in manuscript is 'Harriet' (later used as Mrs Bulstrode's Christian name) and in proof is first changed to 'Helen' and finally to 'Elinor' (Ch. 8). 'Mrs Larcher's' is first 'Mrs Plymdale's' (Ch. 26); 'Billings' is in manuscript changed to 'Oliver' (Ch. 38).

There is one minor change in proof which, though unique, seems worth noting. It slipped by the printer and publisher but not by George Eliot (or Lewes) in reading proof. Casaubon has decided 'to adorn his life with the graces of female companionship' by marrying Dorothea Brooke; the corrected text reads,

Hence he determined to abandon himself to the stream of feeling, and perhaps was surprised to find what an exceedingly shallow rill it was. As in droughty regions baptism by immersion could only be performed symbolically, so Mr Casaubon found that sprinkling was the utmost approach to a plunge which his stream could afford him. . . . (Ch. 7)

In manuscript Casaubon was 'surprised to find what an exceedingly shallow brook it was'.[10]

Among the many changes that go beyond the mechanical or grammatical, beyond spelling and punctuation, and beyond the use of a foreign phrase or its equivalent or the presence or absence of the source for an allusion, are two small but substantive changes—i.e., those that necessitate changing the wording of the text—which may reveal George Eliot's fear that some of her more freethinking language might appear in poor taste to the conventional reader. Tom Cranch has a sense of moral superiority but less aristocratic legs and trousers than Fred Vincy; looking at his legs he 'left it uncertain whether he preferred his moral advantages to a more vicious length of limb, or to the heavenly displeasure at a better cut of trouser', but the last part of this manuscript passage George Eliot changes in proof to, '. . . vicious length of limb and reprehensible gentility of trouser' (Ch. 32). A similar change is made a little later in the novel, though, because we do not have corrected proof for this section, we cannot be certain that it was George Eliot herself who made the change: '[Dagley] read a chapter in the Bible with immense difficulty, *not because he regarded that Ancient Book as somewhat backward, but* because such names as Isaiah or Apollos remained unmanageable after twice spelling' (Ch. 39).[11]

Among the more substantive proof changes are eight that more or less directly involve the presence of the omniscient author in the work. Only one of these involves the addition of a comment; George Eliot adds in proof a parenthetical remark on the first page of Chapter 30 which calls attention to the historicity of the fiction: Lydgate uses a stethoscope, '(which had not become a matter of course in practice at that time)'. A very common and unobtrusive bit of comment, the use of a weighted adjective, is deleted in a passage which is largely devoted to showing Casaubon's view of his relationship to Will and Dorothea: 'but there had entered into the husband's *suspicious* mind the certainty that she judged him . . .' (Ch. 42). Two generalized 'pearls of wisdom' are also eliminated in proof. The first concerns Will's suppression of his image of Dorothea and Casaubon—'beautiful lips kissing holy skulls'—

Also he had to take care that his speech should not betray that thought *—a sort of exercise which determines many things in conversation.* (Ch. 37)

The second is a bit of editorial vituperation against Rosamond, the impulse toward which George Eliot often has difficulty in controlling. Here, she deletes in proof a parenthetical and some-what pontifical judgment and generalization:

'I expect to hear of the marriage', said Rosamond, playfully. (*The essence of stupidity is egoism.*)
     'Never! You will never hear of the marriage!' (Ch. 59)

A third generalization is the more overtly intrusive in that it is put in the first person (plural). From the description of Sir James's chivalrous, brotherly and generous feelings toward Dorothea now that she has married Casaubon, George Eliot has deleted in proof a full sentence of final comment:

In the modern division of labour we must sometimes be contented to get good feelings packed apart from fine ideas and fine rhetoric. (Ch. 29)

She deletes in 1874 proof another, cosier, first-person plural: 'Eighteen months ago *we know that* Lydgate was poor . . .' (Ch. 58), the phrase 'we are aware that' having been first substituted in that proof and then itself deleted. Two further intrusions of the author's voice, these in the first-person singular, are deleted in proof. The first concerned Lydgate's failure to notice Dorothea in the presence of Rosamond: '*I think* the gentleman was too much occupied with the presence of the one woman to reflect on the contrast between the two . . .' (Ch. 43). The other mitigates though it does not eliminate a bit of Trollopian author-to-reader coyness:

Will any one guess towards which of those widely different men Mary had the peculiar woman's tenderness?—the one she was most inclined to be severe on, or the contrary? *I have a notion, but I will not tell.* (Ch. 40)

A modern reader might be tempted at first to infer from such changes that George Eliot was consciously minimizing authorial comment and moving in the direction of the Jamesian novel. A mere eight changes in the proof of a thousand-page novel scarcely

substantiates so sweeping a conclusion, however, especially
when one of the changes in fact adds an authorial comment,
another leaves more comment than it deletes, and a third merely
deletes a weighted adjective. These changes should be seen
instead as operating within the omniscient author convention,
modulating tone and emphasis, adjusting the distance between
the omniscient author and a given character at particular points
in the narration. The remaining substantive revisions in proof
should be considered as functioning within this tradition, many
of them relevant to its proper operation. For convenience, the
revisions will be discussed in groups relating to specific characters or groups of interacting characters.

Except for the elimination of the vituperative comment indicated
earlier, I have found no substantive changes in proof dealing with
Rosamond, and there are remarkably few dealing with Lydgate's
relationship to her or even with Lydgate himself.

The single revision even indirectly involving Rosamond
occurs in a passage in which Lydgate's male-chauvinist view of
the perfect wife is being presented, from which one phrase has
been deleted; he prefers a woman who is

docile, therefore, and ready to carry out behests which came from *the
over-luminous dark of the region* beyond that [womanly] limit. (Ch. 36)

Since this appears in a passage introduced by 'Lydgate thought
that . . .', George Eliot here seems anxious to let Lydgate's
foolish views of women criticize themselves in words which he
himself would use or accept without her introducing overstate-
ment which might border on parody.

A somewhat similar but more subtle adjustment had been
made a few pages earlier. In this passage we are never quite
inside Lydgate's thoughts, though we do move from closer to
less close; a clause explaining his thought processes, which removes us still farther away from him to a position of analysis and
judgment, has been eliminated:

But it had never occurred to him that he should live in any other than
what he would have called an ordinary way, with green glasses for
hock, and excellent waiting at table. *Such things remained an unquestioned*

45

fundamental condition of thought, for in warming himself at French social theories he had brought away no smell of scorching. (Ch. 36)

Lydgate's assumption that middle-class amenities are somehow his due and that life without them is for him virtually unthinkable is one of the chief elements going to make up his 'commonness', and these 'spots of commonness' largely define the pride and egotism which contribute to his downfall.[12] It is easy to forget Lydgate's own share in the financial debacle that overwhelms him; it is not just Rosamond's social pride but his own which leads to the piling up of debts. George Eliot must have thought this was sufficiently emphasized, for she deleted another passage hammering Lydgate's unconscious expectations home. It now reads, 'A house must be taken instead of the rooms he at present occupied; and Lydgate, having heard Rosamond speak . . .'; in manuscript there is much more:

A house must be taken instead of the rooms he at present occupied, and in a provincial place houses must be snapped up when you can get them. Marriages had often been deferred in Middlemarch, from the want of a suitable house, or a young couple not without style themselves had to furnish up a mere journeyman's residence and give it a fallacious appearance of gentility with expensive blinds and a polished door-knocker. Not that such a compromise presented itself as possible to Lydgate: he had no other idea of his establishment in marriage than that everything suitable must and would be rented or bought; and having heard from Rosamond. . . . (Ch. 36)[13]

The final substantive change in the presentation of Lydgate also involves his egocentricity or 'commonness' and the adjustment of point of view. Here the author's ironic—perhaps sarcastic—comment is heightened by the addition of a parenthetical phrase and Lydgate's own comment is put in quotation marks to distinguish it from that of the author:

. . . Captain Lydgate, the baronet's third son, who, I am sorry to say, was detested by our Tertius of that name as a vapid fop parting his hair from brow to nap in a despicable manner and showing an ignorant	. . . Captain Lydgate, the baronet's third son, who, I am sorry to say, was detested by our Tertius of that name as a vapid fop 'parting his hair from brow to nap in a despicable fashion' (not followed by

security that he knew the proper thing to say on every topic.	Tertius himself), and showing an ignorant security that he knew the proper thing to say on every topic.[14]

Except for the spelling out of contractions in representing his speech, there are few substantive revisions in proof which involve Fred Vincy. One of these, however, is the most extensive proof change of all, the addition of an entire scene. As mentioned already, Haight (Riverside Edition, p. 178) indicates the insertion of the scene; he understandably does not detail several minor adjustments that were made necessary by the addition. The added scene actually replaces a brief passage in the manuscript (which appears later in the revised text in a somewhat different form—cf. Ch. 24):

Fred's appearance at this hour surprized [sic] her, but surprize [sic] was not a feeling that she was given to express, and she said very quietly,

'You, Fred! so early in the day. You look quite pale. What has happened? Nothing painful I hope.'

The manuscript continues, 'Yes, Mrs Garth . . . I am come to tell Mr Garth . . .' but, after the intervening scene is added, the proof is adjusted to the present reading: 'Yes, Mr Garth . . . I am come to tell you and Mrs Garth . . .' (Ch. 24). In the next paragraph there is a sentence ending 'without verbal resources', the next beginning, 'Mrs Garth was mutely astonished'. In manuscript the passage reads, '. . . without verbal resources, and not doubting that Mrs Garth knew all. She was mutely astonished.'

In a scene in Chapter 66, Mr Farebrother, Fred's rival for the love of Mary Garth, is in the awkward position of feeling morally obliged to speak against his own self-interest by trying to prevent Fred from slipping back into his bad habits and thus forfeiting Mary's love. Farebrother admits to Fred he was tempted not to interfere, having said to himself,

'. . . If there's a chance of his going to the dogs, let him—perhaps you could nohow hinder it—and do you take the benefit.'

He resists, however: 'But I had once meant better than that, and I am come back to my old intention. . . .' Between his confession of temptation and his triumphing over it, a paragraph describing Fred's reaction is added in proof:

There was a pause in which Fred was seized by a most uncomfortable chill. What was coming next? He dreaded to hear that something had been said to Mary—he felt as if he were listening to a threat rather than a warning. When the Vicar began again there was a change in his tone like the encouraging transition to a major key.[15]

The entire scene is presented from Fred's point of view, so the interpolated paragraph does not constitute a shift. Part of the function of the addition would seem to be to heighten the suspense, or at least Fred's suspense, or to chart more fully his reaction. The chief effect of the revision, however, is not as it relates to Fred but in its punctuating Farebrother's remarks so that the confession and the triumph do not follow each other so immediately: to some degree, then, making Farebrother's self-sacrifice more credible.

George Eliot inserts a lengthy passage into Chapter 52 which seems to have a similar function. In this scene Farebrother feels compelled to plead with Mary Garth on behalf of Fred. In the added passage, however, Farebrother, with perfect probity, removes any guilt feelings Mary may have about her having prevented Fred from inheriting Stone Court—sitting alone with the dying Peter Featherstone she had refused without witnesses to destroy the will which, it turned out, left the estate to Joshua Rigg. Thus he enables Mary to make a clear choice between himself and his rival without her feeling that she need compensate Fred for his material loss. In the manuscript one paragraph ends with Mary saying, '. . . whenever you have anything to say to me I feel honoured', the next begins with Farebrother replying, 'Then I may go on . . .'. Between these passages the following was inserted in proof:

'But before I enter on that question, let me just touch a point on which your father took me into confidence; by the way, it was that very evening on which I once before fulfilled a mission from Fred, just after he had gone to college. Mr Garth told me what happened on the night of Featherstone's death—how you refused to burn the will; and he said that you had some heart-prickings on that subject, because you had been the innocent means of hindering Fred from getting his ten thousand pounds. I have kept that in mind, and I have heard something that may relieve you on that score—may show you that no sin-offering is demanded from you there.'

Mr Farebrother paused a moment and looked at Mary. He meant to give Fred his full advantage, but it would be well, he thought, to clear her mind of any superstitions, such as women sometimes follow when they do a man the wrong of marrying him as an act of atonement. Mary's cheeks had begun to burn a little, and she was mute.

'I mean, that your action made no real difference to Fred's lot. I find that the first will would not have been legally good after the burning of the last; it would not have stood if it had been disputed, and you may be sure it would have been disputed. So, on that score, you may feel your mind free.'

'Thank you, Mr Farebrother', said Mary, earnestly. 'I am grateful to you for remembering my feelings.'

If Farebrother's self-sacrificing goodness is tempered in the revision of the proof, Caleb Garth's moral hardness is softened in the one substantive change in the proof which deals with his presentation. The manuscript describes, 'a striking mixture in him . . . of rigorous demands about workmen and thorough compassion for them'. This seems to suggest one whose feelings are disposed toward sympathy with the workingmen, but whose actions ('demands') are firm. The proof is revised to read: 'a striking mixture in him of rigorous notions about workmen and practical indulgence towards them' (Ch. 31), which suggests one whose theories are harsher than his practice.

The revision of a brief passage dealing with another minor character, Celia Brooke, is more complex in its effect. Celia, with her 'negative wisdom', sees that Sir James Chettam is mistaken in believing Dorothea cares for him, that Dorothea cares only about her 'notions', and that Dorothea, in her rhapsodizing, is often unaware 'that people were staring, not listening'. Celia's concern for appearances, her suspicion of all enthusiasm, her social realism, have all been established with regard to Sir James's illusion and Dorothea's ardour, but they are extended and exemplified in a final sentence in this passage, which, in manuscript reads:

49

When people talked with energy and emphasis she watched their faces and gestures merely, and she never could understand how any one consented to sing and open his mouth in that ridiculous manner.

The social basis of her values is emphasized in proof by the addition of 'well-bred', and the limitations of her views are, perhaps, implied not only in that term but in the apparently mimetic pomposity of a phrase added to the passage:

When people talked with energy and emphasis she watched their faces and features merely. She never could understand how well-bred persons consented to sing and open their mouths in the ridiculous manner requisite for that vocal exercise. (Ch. 3)

Thus a passage which was originally devoted primarily to an ironic view of Dorothea seen from Celia's common-sensical vantage point is now made to turn back on Celia and evaluate her as well, without detracting from the clarity and justice of her criticism of Dorothea.

Most of the changes in proof of the Brooke portions of the novel seem to involve Will Ladislaw and others' relations and reactions to him. Casaubon, sensitive about his own age relative to Ladislaw's youth, corrects first Mr Brooke (Ch. 9) and later Mrs Cadwallader (Ch. 34) when they refer to Will as his nephew. On both occasions in the manuscript Casaubon scrupulously identifies the youth as his 'second cousin', but in the 1874 edition 'second' is both times omitted, the first revision made in proof, the second apparently changed before proof was pulled. George Eliot insists that Casaubon's 'antipathy to Will did not spring from the common jealousy of a winter-worn husband', however; Casaubon's 'uneasy jealousy' was a matter of disposition, and those of us so disposed feel that 'if our talents are chiefly of the burrowing kind, our honey-sipping cousin . . . is likely to have a secret contempt for us, and any one who admires him passes an oblique criticism on ourselves'. It was bad enough while he had been helping Will, 'but he had begun to dislike him still more now that Will had declined his help' (Ch. 37). The end of the paragraph defining this jealousy is revised in proof; I include it for the sake of comprehensiveness, though I am unable to define the precise nature of the change and its effect:

His antipathy to Will did not spring from the common jealousy of a winter-worn husband: it was something deeper, penetrating his life-long associations and claims, but Dorothea, now that she was present—Dorothea, as a young wife who herself had disclosed an offensive capability of criticism, necessarily gave concentration to the previously vague uneasiness.

His antipathy to Will did not spring from the common jealousy of a winter-worn husband: it was something deeper, bred by his lifelong claims and discontents; but Dorothea, now that she was present—Dorothea, as a young wife who herself had shown an offensive capability of criticism, necessarily gave concentration to the uneasiness which had before been vague.

(The change from 'disclosed' to 'shown' perhaps avoids suggesting something vaguely sneaky about Dorothea's newly recognized tendency to criticize.)

A couple of changes in proof seem to have as their purpose the separation of Casaubon's and Sir James's actions against Will. Brooke, standing for Parliament on a platform of Reform, has hired Will to assist him. Casaubon's objection to the arrangement is essentially that it keeps his disliked cousin in the neighbourhood; he is basically in sympathy with Brooke's politics. Sir James's primary objection is, ostensibly, to the indignity of his wife's family being engaged in reformist politics. Casaubon has already forbidden Will to visit Lowick Manor and is 'preparing other measures of frustration'. A paragraph specifying his community of interest with Sir James, though for different reasons, is deleted in proof from near the end of Chapter 37:

It was just possible that Sir James might take some action himself on the ground of political objections, in which Mr Casaubon could not fully join, though he would be glad to see them effective in checking Mr Brooke.

Elimination of this paragraph necessitated a deletion of the opening clause of Chapter 38: '*Mr Casaubon was right in conjecturing that* Sir James could not look with any satisfaction on Mr Brooke's new courses. . . .' The apparent function in separating Casaubon's and Sir James's opposition is to avoid the suggestion that Casaubon, however indirectly, is betraying his political principles to his jealousy. There is another effect, however. George Eliot seems to insist that Sir James's actions toward Dorothea and Will are familial, though it is difficult to avoid seeing Sir James as jealous of Will. Linking Casaubon's jealous and Sir James's political opposition to Will's presence would no doubt in some measure suggest identity of cause as well as identity of interest in the two men's opposition.

There are four changes in passages dealing with Dorothea's reaction to or feelings for Will. In the first, her somewhat excessive reaction to Will's story of his early life is toned down: 'clasping her hands, and turning pale from keen interest' is altered to, 'with keen interest, clasping her hands on her lap' (Ch. 37). In the second, Dorothea, now a widow, is on the verge of realizing her love for Will, though she does not yet fully do so. The manuscript reads, 'She did not know then that it was . . . Love to whom she was sobbing her farewell as his image waned from the mirror of the day.' The waning of the image of Love in the mirror of the day seemed to suggest something too ephemeral about that love which disappeared with first light, or at least something too passive in the agency of daylight; the passage was revised at first in proof to read, 'She did not know then that it was . . . Love to whom she was sobbing her farewell as his image was banished by the day.' Though not further revised in extant proof 'the day' appears in the first edition as 'the insistent day'. In proof of the 1874 edition 'day' is made still more powerful an agent, though not a malevolent one: 'the blameless rigour of irresistible day' (Ch. 55). In the final version the passage begins to approach those 'rude awakening' scenes which Barbara Hardy has pointed out as forming an insistent motif in George Eliot's later novels,[16] though—to the regret of many readers—the disenchantment here is not permanent; Will, or 'Love', returns. The third change renders one of the several scenes between Will and Dorothea a bit more aseptic by deleting the clause from the manuscript version which describes their touching: 'As Mrs Kell closed the door behind her they met; *but neither of them spoke a word while their hands were joined for an instant*: each was looking at the other, and consciousness was overflowed by something that suppressed utterance' (Ch. 62).

Finally, there is some tinkering with the description of Dorothea's feelings as she prepares to go to Rosamond:

This habitual swathe of feeling about Will Ladislaw had formed part of all her waking hours since she had proposed to go and see Mrs Lydgate . . .	This habitual state of feeling about Will Ladislaw had been strong in all her waking hours since she had proposed to pay a visit to Mrs Lydgate . . . (Ch. 77)

At first in proof 'swathe' was deleted in favour of 'pulse', but even that was apparently a bit too emotive. (The phrase 'go and see' was not revised until proof of the 1874 edition.)

Mrs Farebrother tells Dorothea that Henrietta Noble, when she 'forms an attachment to anyone . . . is like a dog—she would take their shoes for a pillow and sleep the better'. Miss Noble, in a sentence added to the proof, is forced to confirm the hyperbole—'"Mr Ladislaw's shoes, I would", said Henrietta Noble' (Ch. 80)—an addition which raises neither Will nor Miss Noble in the reader's estimation.

Fortunately, Will's effeminacy, still offensive to many critics, is qualified slightly by revision of the proof. What seems dubious enough in its final version—'his bright curls and delicate but rather petulant profile, with its defiant curves of lip and chin' (Ch. 37)—read in manuscript, 'his bright curls and delicate but rather petulant profile, in which the defiant curves of lip and chin were scarcely shaded by hair even of the shaven sort'.

Less fortunate is the deletion of one of the few ironic references to Will. He is being torn between approval of Dorothea's 'duteous preoccupation' with Casaubon and torment at 'that gentleman's sandy absorption of such nectar' (changed in proof to 'the husband's sandy absorption', perhaps toning down Will's contempt but also suggesting to some degree that it is Casaubon's role as Dorothea's husband that irks Will). The ironic sentence that ended the paragraph is deleted: 'Gentlemen waiting for their genius to declare itself have time for this kind of inward drama' (Ch. 22).

The ten pages or so in Chapter 61 which deal with Bulstrode's state of mind with regard to Raffles—who had recently revisited Middlemarch—and which prepare for Bulstrode's later spiritual struggle which eventuates in his virtually murdering Raffles, are more extensively revised in proof than is any other section of the novel. Many of these changes can be seen as technical adjustments of point of view—there are a number, for example, which eliminate first-person plural commentary—but the main burden of the changes seems to be more moral than technical, an attempt to get us to understand Bulstrode from within rather than merely to forgive him because we are all sinners.

A number of the changes in this passage stress the terror and pain of his situation, part of the pain being the absence of pleasure in Bulstrode's looking back on his past. Bulstrode is sure that 'Raffles—unless providence sent death to hinder him—would come back to Middlemarch before long'; the next sentence is added in proof: 'And that certainty was a terror'. By the intensification of the rhythm of the sentences and the addition of the 'smarting' and the loss of pleasure, Bulstrode's misery is further heightened for the reader by changes in the next two paragraphs:

intense memory forces a man to own his blameworthy past, not simply as a dead history, an outworn preparation of the present, a repented error shaken loose from the life—rather as a still quivering part of himself bringing shudders and bitter flavours and the tinglings of a merited shame.

intense memory forces a man to own his blameworthy past. With memory set smarting like a re-opened wound, a man's past is not simply a dead history, an outworn preparation of the present. It is not a repented error shaken loose from the life. It is a still quivering part of himself bringing shudders and bitter flavours and the tinglings of a merited shame.[17]

Bulstrode's memory was in this condition. Night and day . . .

Into this second life Bulstrode's past had now risen, only the pleasures of it seeming to have lost their quality. Night and day . . .

In manuscript, his 'shrinking' from engaging in the shady pawn-broker's business is 'overcome' by argument and prayer, but the proof rewords the passage so as to leave the possible implication that the shrinking remains, even though he does decide to continue in the business:

He remembered the first moments of shrinking, but the shrinking was private, and was overcome by arguments; some of these taking the form of prayer.	He remembered the first moments of shrinking. They were private, and were filled with arguments; some of these taking the form of prayer.

Bulstrode's present discomfort is kept before the reader by the change of 'memory' to 'burning memory', and a little later the 'unusually worn look' on his face is changed to 'the painfully worn look'. In a more extensive change in this chapter, Bulstrode's 'conflict' is described as 'spiritual', and his 'dread' and 'need' and the difficulty of his resolution are added, further stressing the painfulness of his situation and obviating the possible inference that he is easily choosing the easy path:

He had been fortunate enough to see Raffles actually going away on the Brassing coach, and this was a temporary relief, but it made little difference to the hidden conflict, which issued in a letter to Will Ladislaw . . .	He had seen Raffles actually going away on the Brassing coach, and this was a temporary relief; it removed the pressure of an immediate dread, but did not put an end to the spiritual conflict and the need to win protection. At last he came to a difficult resolve, and wrote a letter to Will Ladislaw . . .

George Eliot's revision of proof in Chapter 61 not only emphasizes Bulstrode's dread, pain and difficulty in rationalizing his conduct, but also the pleasure he gets from his recent position of power and thus implies the intensity of the loss with which he is now threatened. Even more important in the expansion of the following sentence of manuscript is the shift from what we might be more likely to call his belief 'in his own piety' to what he calls belief 'in the peculiar work of Grace within him':

The distinction and power of Brother Bulstrode were locally narrow, but they were the more intensely felt; he believed without effort in his own piety, and in the signs that God intended him for special instrumentality.	The people among whom Brother Bulstrode was distinguished were very few, but they were very near to him and stirred his satisfaction the more; his power stretched through a narrow space, but he felt its effect the more intensely. He believed without effort in the peculiar work of Grace within him, and in the signs that God intended him for special instrumentality.[18]

A similar change involves Bulstrode's 'prayer' which in the manuscript is baldly self-seeking—'I am sinful and nought—a vessel to be consecrated by use—but serve me!'—but which, by the substitution in proof of 'use' for 'serve', is made more consistent with Bulstrode's self-deceiving rationalization of his religion; in effect, 'Let Thy will be done (but may Thy will be my will)'.[19]

The precise effect of the revisions involving the editorial 'we' is somewhat difficult to assess. One such change seems to do little more than substitute a third-person singular form in the generalization:

But if we believe in something else than our own greed, we have necessarily a conscience and standard to which we try more or less to adapt ourselves.	But a man who believes in something else than his own greed, has necessarily a conscience or standard to which he more or less adapts himself.

Another such revision clearly shifts the focus from the general to the specific case of Bulstrode:

When we settle what is due from us to others by inquiring what are God's intentions with regard to ourselves conclusions are not narrowly restricted.	It was easy for him to settle what was due from him to others by inquiring what were God's intentions with regard to himself.

A third revised passage does not completely eliminate the first-person plural, though a long sentence in first-person plural which departs from the specifics of Bulstrode's thought is deleted, and, earlier in the passage, 'seemed' is changed to the more concrete 'he thought'. It may be worth quoting two full paragraphs here to show both the careful reworking of the first paragraph and the context of the more important deletion of the final sentence, especially since this is a key passage in the vexed question of Bulstrode's 'hypocrisy':

Meanwhile something which he had learned in his conversation with Raffles entered actively into the struggle of his longings and terrors, and seemed to open at least some spiritual — perhaps some material rescue.

Meanwhile, in his conversation with Raffles, he had learned something momentous, something which entered actively into the struggle of his longings and terrors. There, he thought, lay an opening towards spiritual, perhaps towards material rescue.

The spiritual kind of rescue was a genuine need for him. There may be coarse hypocrites who consciously affect beliefs and emotions for the sake of gulling the world, but Bulstrode was not one of them. He was simply a man whose desires had been stronger than his theoretic beliefs and who had gradually explained the gratification of his desires into satisfactory agreement with those beliefs; a process which shows itself occasionally in us all, to whatever confession we belong, and whether we believe in the future perfection of our race or in the nearest date fixed for the end of the world, whether we regard the earth as a putrefying nidus for a saved remnant in-

The spiritual kind of rescue was a genuine need for him. There may be coarse hypocrites, who consciously affect beliefs and emotions for the sake of gulling the world, but Bulstrode was not one of them. He was simply a man whose desires had been stronger than his theoretic beliefs, and who had gradually explained the gratification of his desires into satisfactory agreement with those beliefs. If this be hypocrisy, it is a process which shows itself occasionally in us all, to whatever confession we belong, and whether we believe in the future perfection of our race or in the nearest date fixed for the end of the world; whether we regard the earth as a putrefying nidus for

57

cluding ourselves or have a passionate belief in the solidarity of mankind. But the inconsistency common to man may vary from the sleeve-worn humours which make us ridiculous to the secret commission, the sophistical self-justification and the indirect atonement keeping clear of betrayal which make a tragic experience roughly branded with the ready-made lettering hypocrisy.

a saved remnant, including ourselves, or have a passionate belief in the solidarity of mankind.

The extended appeal to 'us' to identify our relatively harmless inconsistencies with those of Bulstrode, while apparently meant to help us sympathise with him, courts the danger of worsening his offences: to make ourselves ridiculous through 'sleeve-worn humours' is, after all, considerably less socially harmful or immoral than his justification of past actions that bordered on the criminal, which is to lead finally to the very verge of murder.

The revision of the proof of this portion of the novel not only keeps us more concretely aware of Bulstrode's dread and pain and of the process by which this pious, self-consciously moral man can yield to temptation without facing the true nature or consequences of his thoughts and actions, but also, though lessening the frequency of direct appeals to our sympathies, increases our sympathy by increasing our understanding. The original version of this section of Chapter 61, by more frequently dragging the reader in, asks him to judge Bulstrode tolerantly—but to judge him; since most of us, presumably, have not erred precisely as Bulstrode did, not, perhaps, quite so seriously, this judgment will be handed down from the foothills if not the heights of moral superiority. The revised version, forcing us, for the most part, to see through his eyes, calls not for judgment but for the realization of how he could see his immoral actions in a different if admittedly somewhat murky light; it invites a willing suspension of moral righteousness.

Some of the tendencies in the extensive revision of Chapter 61 may be seen in certain minor changes made in Chapter 70, in which Bulstrode finally yields to his greatest temptation. When Mrs Abel comes to the door of Bulstrode's room to ask if she cannot give Raffles brandy, contrary to the orders Lydgate had left with him and he with Mrs Abel, 'To her surprise, Mr Bulstrode did not answer. A struggle *which took the form of an argument* was going on within him.' Apparently in this deletion, as in the revision of the 'shrinking' passage quoted earlier, there is an attempt to play down the consciousness, the rationality of the process which leads Bulstrode to give in to his desires. As George Eliot asks a few paragraphs later, 'who', even in prayer, 'can represent himself just as he is, even in his own reflections?' And, she adds, 'Bulstrode had not yet unravelled in his thought the confused promptings of the last four-and-twenty hours'. No doubt to keep before us the wearing effect of the struggle on Bulstrode, she added in proof the word here enclosed in parenthesis in the following climatic sentence: 'Here a key was thrust through the inch of door-way, and Mr Bulstrode said (huskily), "That is the key of the wine-cooler."'

Perhaps the most significant revision of a brief passage from the time of the completion of the manuscript to the 1874 version of the novel is that of the last two paragraphs of the 'Finale', which deal with the Dorothea-Theresa theme. Haight (River-side Edition, p. 612) indicates the chief change in the penultimate paragraph, that made between the first and 1874 editions. He does not print, however, the earliest version, that of the manuscript (proof of the Finale is missing, though it may be assumed that the differences between the uncorrected manuscript and the first edition were the result of changes made in proof). It may be well to print all three versions here, in chronological sequence, from manuscript, first edition and 1874 edition:

Certainly those determining acts of her life were not ideally beautiful. They were the mixed result of young and noble impulse struggling with imperfect conditions. Among the many criticisms which passed on her first marriage nobody remarked that it could not have happened if she had not been born into a society which smiled on propositions of marriage from a sickly man to a girl less than half his own age, and, in general, encouraged the view that to renounce an advantage to oneself which might be got from the folly or ignorance of others is a sign of mental weakness. While this tone of opinion is part of the social medium in which young creatures begin to breathe, there will be collisions such as those in Dorothea's life, where great feelings will take the aspect of error, and great faith the aspect of illusion. For there is no creature whose inward being is so strong that it is not greatly determined by what lies outside it. It is not likely that a new Theresa will have the opportunity of reforming a conventual life . . . .

Certainly those determining acts of her life were not ideally beautiful. They were the mixed result of young and noble impulse struggling under prosaic conditions. Among the many remarks passed on her mistakes, it was never said in the neighbourhood of Middlemarch that such mistakes could not have happened if the society into which she was born had not smiled on propositions of marriage from a sickly man to a girl less than half his own age—on modes of education which make a woman's knowledge another name for motley ignorance—on rules of conduct which are in flat contradiction with its own loudly-asserted beliefs. While this is the social air in which mortals begin to breathe, there will be collisions such as those in Dorothea's life, where great feelings will take the aspect of error, and great faith the aspect of illusion. For there is no creature whose inward being is so strong that it is not greatly determined by what lies outside it. A new Theresa will hardly have the opportunity of reforming a conventual life. . . .

Certainly those determining acts of her life were not ideally beautiful. They were the mixed result of young and noble impulse struggling amidst the conditions of an imperfect social state, in which great feelings will often take the aspect of error, and great faith the aspect of illusion. For there is no creature whose inward being is so strong that it is not greatly determined by what lies outside it. A new Theresa will hardly have the opportunity of reforming a conventual life. . . .

The manuscript version centres on Dorothea's first marriage and the local criticism of that marriage. It descends from the generalization of 'young and noble impulse struggling with imperfect conditions' to the marriage in particular and criticizes the society for smiling on that marriage, then moves to the general proposition that the society encourages its members to take advantage of one another's ignorance and folly, as, by implication, Casaubon took advantage of Dorothea. The first edition specifies that that marriage was a 'mistake'. It adds to the indictment of society specifically the shortcomings of female education and more sweepingly the breeding of hypocrisy (rules of conduct contrary to professed beliefs).

The final version, on the other hand, is even more generalized than the first, markedly more so than the second. It omits all mention of Dorothea's first marriage, the attack on the short-comings of the education of women, the advocacy by society of taking advantage of others, and even the discrepancy between rules of conduct and professed beliefs. The last sentence of the paragraph in all versions—'But we insignificant people with our daily words and acts are preparing the lives of many Dorotheas, some of which may present a far sadder sacrifice than that of the Dorothea whose story we know'—still suggests a basically meliorist position: i.e., that our moral choices will to some degree effect human history, so that the better we are individually the better to that extent our society as a whole will be. The elimination of all mention of the specific social or socio-moral ills, from inadequate female education to moral hypocrisy, leaving only the struggle between great feelings and faith against 'the conditions of an imperfect social state', while it universalizes the moral statement, moves that statement from a tough-minded but moderately hopeful meliorism toward a tragic view of the human condition. For the imperfect social state, we must assume, will always be with us. With no marauding dragons to attack—like hypocrisy and lack of adequate educa-tional opportunities for women—the thrust of the paragraph is toward resignation, perhaps with a sigh. This is more congenial to the modern sensibility though I am not so sure it as adequately suggests the moral vision of the novel.[20]

The revision of the final sentence of the novel—changed between manuscript and first edition, presumably in proof—points in the same direction as that of the final revision of the preceding paragraph:

But the effect of her being on those around her was incalculably diffusive: for the growing life of the world is after all chiefly dependent on unhistoric acts,	But the effect of her being on those around her was incalculably diffusive: for the growing good of the world is partly dependent on unhistoric acts; and that

and that things are not so ill with you and me as they might have been is owing to many of those who sleep in unvisited tombs, having lived a hidden life nobly.	things are not so ill with you and me as they might have been is half owing to the number who lived faithfully a hidden life, and rest in unvisited tombs.

It does not seem fanciful to say that the difference in tone of the two versions of the Finale may be summed up in the difference between the final words. After a thousand and more pages, the reader of the manuscript ends *Middlemarch* on the word 'nobly', the reader of the novel on the word 'tombs'. The emphasis of the earlier version seems to be upon the individual's duty to try, at least, to live his life nobly and, perhaps infinitesimally, to make things 'not so ill' for those who will follow. The published version gives only half the credit for our relative well being to those who struggled nobly but who now rest in 'unvisited tombs'.

4

The Language of the Novel
The Character of Dorothea

DEREK OLDFIELD

THERE are critics who have felt impelled to patronise George
Eliot's style. Her manner, said W. C. Brownell, was often not
'felicitous'. 'It is inspired by the wish to be pointed, to be
complete, to give an impeccable equivalent in expression for the
content of thought, to be adequately articulate.' We might think
that this was high praise, but not so. 'She has no style. . . . She
was the slave of the meaning. . . . Every sentence stands by
itself; by its sententious self.' The direction of the attack is
interesting. George Eliot has apparently not decked 'the sense
as if it were to sell'. She has actually—appalling fault—allowed
her ideas to contaminate her expression: 'The manner naturally
takes on the character of the substance, and we have thus the
formal sententiousness—now epigrammatic, as I say, and now
otiose and obscure—because of the writer's exclusive consecration to the content, which itself varies, of course, from the
pithy to the commonplace.'[1] It would seem reasonable to object
to consecration to a content which we hold unworthy of devotion.
But Brownell does not object: 'no other novelist gives one such a
poignant, sometimes such an insupportable, sense that life is
immensely serious, and no other, in consequence, is surer of
being read and read indefinitely, by serious readers.'[2] In other
words Brownell is finding George Eliot wanting in that she says
just what she intends to say without the embellishments of 'style'.

In 1861, however, George Eliot was attacked for *not* convey-
ing her intended meaning. The reviewer in *Macmillan's Magazine* declared that *he* had respect for Tom Tulliver even if George
Eliot had none.

This aspersion on the gulf between effect and intended effect
in her writing George Eliot passionately rebutted: 'as if it were
not *my* respect for Tom which infused itself into my reader—as
if he could have respected Tom, if I had not painted him with
respect.'[3] Even Vernon Lee could seem to know George Eliot's
intention better than George Eliot herself: 'She conveys a wrong
impression of characters whom, considered analytically, she
understood thoroughly . . . George Eliot's scientific dreariness
of vocabulary and manner of exposition explains very largely
why her professed *charmeurs* and *charmeuse*, Tito, Rosamond
Vincy, Stephen Guest, are so utterly the reverse of charming.
They are correctly thought out as mere analyses, and never do
anything psychologically false or irrelevant; but they are wrongly
expressed.'[4] I should like in this essay to show how advisable it
is to pause a moment before accusing George Eliot of wrong
expression.

Twentieth-century critics tend to agree with Brownell, in
alleging that she makes her intentions all *too* clear. The criticism
lies at the back of Walter Allen's comment: 'George Eliot tells
us much more, in her own voice, about her characters than any
modern novelist would. It is she who tells us what they think and
feel, and she comments on their thinking and feeling; she passes
judgement on them continually. . . .'[5] David Cecil also alludes
to George Eliot's 'dissected' characters who cannot speak for
themselves because of her omnipresent, censorious commentary
—'George Eliot does confront human nature a little like a
school teacher'.[6]

It would be truer to say, however, that criticism itself seems
to have acted the schoolteacher with George Eliot. If we wish to
heighten our appreciation of any work of art, we must abandon
what we fondly believe to be 'absolute' standards of good style
and commit ourselves to a sympathetic understanding of the
pervasive quality of the particular manner we are presented with.
To the Brownells and Cecils, one wants to adapt Lydgate's
retort to *his* detached critic: 'And to say that you love me
without loving the medical man in me, is the same sort of thing
as to say that you like eating a peach but don't like its flavour'
(Ch. 46). To say that you love *Middlemarch* without loving its

64

style. . . . It is the Rosamonds of the literary world who stand apart describing, in Fred Vincy's phrase, the sensations in their own noses.

George Eliot's own one 'absolute' criterion in matters of style was that the words should adequately express the thought. She wrote to John Chapman in 1855:

You have plenty of *thoughts*, and what you have to aim at is the simple, clear expression of those thoughts, dismissing from your mind all efforts after any other qualities than precision and force—any other result than the *complete presentation* of your idea. It would be the best possible symptom in you if your sentences became rather rugged. It would prove that you no longer introduced words for the sake of being *flowing*.[7]

In order to demonstrate this functional nature of style in *Middlemarch* and to counter the two basic criticisms of George Eliot—that her expression does not convey her intended meaning, or that it conveys her meaning all too obviously, that we never get away from the author's voice to hear either the characters themselves or to form our own independent interpretation of the action—I must show that there *is* a very precise intended meaning which George Eliot is communicating, but that she does not communicate it directly. She never semaphores her intention.

Is there any one function that we can all agree George Eliot's style intends to fulfil? In the case of *Middlemarch* we can safely assume that one of her concerns will be to present to us an image of Dorothea. As we learn in the Finale, an appreciation of the importance of 'our daily words and acts' in 'preparing the lives of many Dorotheas' will depend upon our assessment of what Middlemarch did to 'the Dorothea whose story we know'. Before we can appreciate a 'far sadder sacrifice' we have to sympathise with hers.

George Eliot uses three different stylistic methods in her presentation of Dorothea. First, there is her allegedly 'direct' narrator's voice; then there is the dramatization of Dorothea's own speech; and finally there is George Eliot's method of communicating Dorothea's thoughts. How direct is George

Eliot's own voice in *Middlemarch*? Unlike the bungling players at Elsinore, she does not 'tell all'. Her judgments are constantly modified or restricted in some way, whether by such devices as the 'impersonal' narrator, the use of negatives and irony, or by a modifying context.

Sometimes, for example, George Eliot forces us to reserve our acquiescence to some proposition by making it the responsibility of somebody other than herself. We see Dorothea through the eyes of 'Those who approached her' (Ch. 1). We hear what 'Most men' (Ch. 1) thought about her, or what 'all people, young or old that is, in those ante-reform times' (Ch. 3) would have thought of her. We are told what the 'rural opinion about the new young ladies' (Ch. 1) was. Or George Eliot will simply use the passive voice and will write of Dorothea: 'She was usually spoken of as being remarkably clever' (Ch. 1), or 'She was regarded as an heiress' (Ch. 1). On another occasion, George Eliot does not tell us what Dorothea's face expresses, but writes: 'Dorothea's brow took an expression of reprobation and pity' (Ch. 4). George Eliot carefully disavows responsibility for what Dorothea actually felt. All we know is that she pulled the appropriate face. The complexity of things may also be mirrored stylistically when something is first stated and then immediately qualified: 'But perhaps no persons then living—certainly none in the neighbourhood of Tipton. . . ' (Ch. 3). More often still this restrictive effect is achieved by negatives. Similarly, George Eliot's irony often defines by negation:

A young lady of some birth and fortune, who knelt suddenly down on a brick floor by the side of a sick labourer and prayed fervidly as if she thought herself living in the time of the Apostles—who had strange whims of fasting like a Papist and of sitting up at night to read old theological books! (Ch. 1)

The sarcasm directed at the 'young lady' is unmistakable. The whole sentence structure, lacking a finite verb, suggests a proposition to be rejected. Then, too, there are the depreciative 'whims', 'Papist' and the attribution of 'old' to the theological books. There is the incongruous collocation of 'a young lady of some birth and fortune' with 'a brick floor'. Finally there is the frank imputation of delusion, behaving 'as if she thought herself living in the time of the Apostles'. But although the sarcastic tone is unmistakable, the reader is conscious of not identifying himself with the ironic point of view. The past that Dorothea might appear to live in is, after all, the time of the Apostles who claimed a universal relevance for their behaviour; perhaps young ladies and brick floors can respectably come into contact with each other through prayer. Once the critical process has begun, the reader begins to revalue many of the sneers expressed and to realize that it is merely the invalid opinion of a nameless frightened young squire. This modifying process is similar to the effect George Eliot achieves in the opening sentences of *Middlemarch*, defining Miss Brooke's kind of beauty. In fact, instead of telling us directly what to think, George Eliot frequently just tells us what we may *not* think—or lets us oscillate between one attitude that needs qualifying and another. George Eliot, herself, describes the process: 'starting a long way off the true point, and proceeding by loops and zigzags, we now and then arrive just where we ought to be' (Ch. 3). The voice of the narrator seems to make a succession of probes at the truth, observing of Dorothea that she was: 'likely to seek martyrdom, to make retractions and then to incur martyrdom after all in a quarter where she had not sought it' (Ch. 3). Or else the author's voice may be the one fixed bearing to guide the reader in his zig-zags. Let us take a longer passage which starts with one such fixed point of author statement:

She was open, ardent and not in the least self-admiring; indeed it was pretty to see how her imagination adorned her sister Celia with attractions altogether superior to her own, and if any gentleman appeared to come to the Grange from some other motive than that of seeing Mr Brooke, she concluded that he must be in love with Celia: Sir James Chettam, for example, whom she constantly considered from Celia's point of view, inwardly debating whether it would be good for Celia to accept him. That he should be regarded as a suitor to herself would have seemed to her a ridiculous irrelevance. Dorothea, with all her eagerness to know the truths of life, retained very childlike ideas about marriage. She felt sure she would have accepted the judicious Hooker, if she had been born in time to save him from that wretched mistake he made in matrimony; or John Milton when his blindness had come on; or any of the other great men whose odd habits it would have been glorious piety to endure; but an amiable handsome baronet, who said 'Exactly' to her remarks even when she expressed uncertainty,—how could he affect her as a lover? The really delightful marriage must be that where your husband was a sort of father, and could teach you even Hebrew, if you wished it. (Ch. 1)

Nothing could be more authoritative than 'She was open, ardent, and not in the least self-admiring', and the comment which follows, with its pretence of observed reality 'it was pretty to see how. . . .' Then again, after the earlier ambivalent discussion of Dorothea's marriage prospects, the responsibility for remaining single is now firmly made Dorothea's: 'Dorothea, with all her eagerness to know the truths of life, retained very childlike ideas about marriage.' This is immediately followed by a passage which sounds as if it might be a dramatization of Dorothea's consciousness. Here, as often elsewhere, it is introduced by a tag that ambiguously can announce either *oratio recta* or *oratio obliqua*: 'She felt. . . .' That Dorothea's feelings are presented in *oratio recta* is suggested by the slightly collo-quial nature of what follows. '*That wretched* mistake' sounds like a personal voice. Other things being equal, the personal voice claims our sympathy. But one resource of the ironist is to give us the revaluing shock by playing unacceptable ideas off against the plausible voice.

George Eliot leads us into the unacceptable idea by three statements of mounting preposterousness. Hooker, who, according to Izaak Walton, chose an unsuitable wife because his vision (like Dorothea's and Milton's) was faulty, is a less celebrated example of a 'difficult husband' than is Milton; and in the final phase the anti-romantic indiscriminate nature of the selection is made explicit in the universal 'any of the other great men. . .', with the characteristically restrictive addition, 'whose odd habits it would have been glorious piety to endure'. So too it was not Milton at any time whom Dorothea could have regarded as a suitor but 'John Milton when his blindness had come on'. One way in which George Eliot presents Dorothea's thought is by granting her this precision of expression which, when it expresses her delusions, is of course quite cruelly accurate. We know the precise quality of Dorothea's delusions partly because she can express them herself. Part of the tragedy of Dorothea in these early chapters is conveyed by this quality of her thinking that we feel in its accuracy to come so near uncovering its own wrong-headedness. Irony often depends upon incongruous collocations and here there is a very strong stylistic presumption against it being 'glorious piety' to endure 'odd habits': and what right had the 'judicious' Hooker to be making mistakes? The plausible voice continues, 'but an amiable handsome baronet, who said 'Exactly' to her remarks, even when she expressed uncertainty, —how could he affect her as a lover?' Any sympathy we might have had for Sir James, in reaction to Hooker and Milton, is dispelled by the conclusive nature of this report. It has the finality of a Jane Austen sentence: appeal is unthinkable. We move to Dorothea. But the accuracy of the concluding statement appals us. 'The really delightful marriage must be that where your husband was a sort of father, and could teach you even Hebrew, if you wished it.' The candour, the openness is expressed and the contradictory elements brought together so as to be equated 'husband . . . a sort of father'. It is difficult to say whether Dorothea is sensing that she has discovered a paradox or whether there is a frightening suggestion that she is not seeing what to others is 'quite plain'. At all events, we again react away from Dorothea, this time in pity. And this one paragraph shows, I hope, that George Eliot's presentation of Dorothea is very far from imposed didacticism—the reader has to respond to the text with the closest possible attention if he is to react accurately to the multiple points of view, including Dorothea's own distorted view of herself. Already in what is apparently plain narrative description we have a hint of the ventriloquist's art.

In tracing the 'zig-zag' of the reader's sympathy throughout the above-quoted passage, I assumed that it was Dorothea's own voice we were hearing. Yet such an assumption begs many questions. It has not always been allowed that George Eliot differentiates her characters' speech. Yet she herself claimed the 'happiness of being able to recall beloved faces and *accents* with great clearness',[8] and her letters and notebooks record vital interest in dialect and current speech forms. Behind such interest, there is a whole philosophy of directness, a faith in fidelity to 'substantial reality'.[9] In her search for this precision, George Eliot strove in all her novels to be absolutely accurate about current usage in the spoken language. Thus we find her correcting an overzealous proof-reader with real sharpness. She wrote to John Blackwood:

> By today's post I return the proof of Part 2. Part 1 was printed as I wished in every respect except one. The printer's reader made a correction after I saw the proof, and though he may sometimes do so with advantage, as I am very liable to overlook mistakes, I in this case particularly object to his alteration, and I mention it in order to request that it may not occur again. He has everywhere substituted the form— 'the Misses So and So' for the 'Miss So and So's'—a form which in England is confined to public announcements, to the backs of letters, and to the conversation of schoolmistresses. It is not the conversational English of good society, and causes the most disagreeable jolt in an easy style of narrative or description.[10]

Her linguistic accuracy extends to pronunciation, providing evidence of an acute auditory imagination. In her next letter to Blackwood on the subject of proof-reading she writes about *Adam Bede*:

> let me beg of you to mention to the superintendent of your printing office, that in case of another reprint of 'Adam', I beg the word 'sperrit' (for 'spirit') may be particularly attended to. Adam never said 'speerit', as he is made to do in the cheaper edition, at least in one place—his speech at the birthday dinner. This is a small matter, but it is a point I care about.[11]

This interest in the spoken language is often recorded in the journals and letters. Thus she records the Thames Boatman saying about the spring tides, 'tries a fellow, them does'.[12] Or the anonymous Devonian who told Lewes and her that they were 'tu mile' from Ilfracombe.[13] Or, on the same holiday, she will note the 'supererogatory aspirates' of the Town Crier, talking about 'Hironsides, the American Wonder.'[14]

George Henry Lewes was the first critic to value her power of reproducing spoken language. In a letter to Blackwood, he wrote about *Scenes of Clerical Life*: 'It struck me as being fresher than any story I have read for a long while, and as exhibiting in a high degree that faculty which I find to be the rarest of all, viz. the dramatic ventriloquism.'[15] It appears that one of her difficulties in writing *Romola* was not just that her power of 'dramatic ventriloquism' was of no help to her, but that it was a positive embarrassment. John Blackwood refers to this difficulty in a letter to his wife: 'Her great difficulty seems to be that she, as she describes it, hears her characters talking and there is a weight upon her mind as if Savonarola and friends ought to be speaking Italian instead of English. Her description of how she realised her characters was very marvellous.'[16]

If to George Eliot's claims that she could hear her characters talking we add her admiration of that art which dared 'to be thoroughly familiar'[17] (i.e. colloquial), it is not surprising that there is so much dramatic ventriloquism in *Middlemarch*. The characters are not mere spokesmen for the wise, witty and tender sayings of George Eliot—they are other people whom she could hear expressing their own thoughts, in other words, voicing *relative* truths. Even a generally admirable figure like Dorothea is herself, not George Eliot, and must not be regarded uncritically as an absolute. George Eliot herself was irritated by her critics' inability to understand this aspect of her relation to her characters; they make no allowance for the dramatic voice. She answers John Blackwood's early criticism of *Scenes of Clerical Life*:

I think you have rather mistaken the intention of the jokes in the play-bill. They are not meant by any means as Attic wit, but as Milby wit, and any really fine sarcasm would be out of place.[18]

In a short study it is difficult to demonstrate just how skilfully George Eliot provides the people in Middlemarch with an idiom which is an extremely sensitive register of their natures. Bulstrode has evolved a highly efficient means of concealing himself; his abstract and infinitive predicates are nebulous, his constant prepositional phrases conceal connections and weaken his utterances. He is reluctant to use transitive verbs, but relies, with countless qualifications on weak verbs and the copula. Lydgate, the scientist, has a clarity of expression which, through sentence structure and metaphor, lucidly juxtaposes propositions. Casaubon, the 'scholar', accumulates pieces of language, moving further and further from his main clause. Casaubon, the inadequate human being, has 'not two styles of speaking at command', but is strangled by the measured public voice he has developed. His powers of communication have completely atrophied. In his researches, he cannot publish; in meeting other people, he cannot seek for a common idiom, and we watch him grow ever more isolated. Fred Vincy's unpretentious speech ('Oh, fudge!') establishes his basically genuine nature, whilst Mr Brooke's evasive, muddled half-finished speeches are a perfect 'organ' for the politician manqué.

George Eliot does not concern herself exclusively with the psychology of grammar and diction but she is also at great pains to make us 'realize' her characters in *Middlemarch*, through descriptions of their voices and intonation. Trumbull, 'the admirer by nature' (Ch. 60), has a rising intonation, whereas Rosamond's voice, we are told, and we may see if we care to look, 'fell and trickled like cold water drops' (Ch. 64). Dorothea's speech is often like a 'recitative' (Ch. 5) or it has a 'bird-like modulation' (Ch. 22). Lydgate has a voice 'habitually deep and sonorous, yet capable of becoming very low and gentle at the right moment' (Ch. 13). Will has a 'light voice' (Ch. 49), Celia a 'quiet guttural' (Ch. 55), Mrs Garth has a 'deep contralto' (Ch. 56), Mrs Waule a 'woolly tone' (Ch. 32), and Captain Lydgate a 'rather heavy utterance' (Ch. 58). There are many other examples.

Some of these voices are described as changing in different situations. Dorothea's voice can take on a 'melancholy cadence' (Ch. 44), and Fred's 'a tone of grumbling remonstrance' (Ch. 52), and Will's 'a hoarse undertone extremely unlike his usual light voice' (Ch. 49). Rosamond, on the other hand, never 'raised her voice' (Ch. 58), and Celia can be outrageously insensitive 'without the least change of tone' (Ch. 50).

These tones matter if we are to imagine George Eliot's characters accurately. They matter, too, in understanding the relationships established between the characters themselves. It is clear that a highly significant distinction is made between Rosamond and Dorothea, and that this distinction has been conceived in terms of sensitivity of utterance. Thus, Lydgate remembers Dorothea's 'tones of emotion' (Ch. 58), when she cried: '—think what I can do—'

That voice of deep-souled womanhood had remained within him as the enkindling conception of dead and sceptred genius had remained with him . . . the tones were a music from which he was falling away—he had really fallen into a momentary doze, when Rosamond said in her silvery neutral way, 'Here is your tea, Tertius.' (Ch. 58)

She throws the same 'neutrality' into her later words, echoing with significant difference of tone the words of Dorothea, 'What can *I* do, Tertius?'

One might go on indefinitely, but there is little value in merely asserting that George Eliot saw speech as a psychological as well as a social correlative in the presentation of her characters. Let us at least try to demonstrate the value of attending to these nuances of manner of speech in the case of Dorothea. What does such a study reveal about her personality? Might not the changing style of her speech even help to define in what her 'sad sacrifice' consists?

Before her marriage to Casaubon, Dorothea's speech is shown to be in many respects simple. Her ideas succeed each other in a series of short sentences.

'You must not judge of Celia's feelings from mine. I think she likes these small pets. She had a tiny terrier once, which she was very fond of. It made me unhappy because I was afraid of treading on it. I am rather short-sighted.' (Ch. 3)

If ever two people were stylistically incompatible, they are Dorothea and Casaubon. Dorothea makes no attempt to incorporate her subordinate clauses into her statements but leaves them in the position in which they occurred to her in the excited vigour of her thought. 'And then I should know what to do, when I got older' (Ch. 3). Her speech is repetitive. Sometimes, it is true, she seems to be striving for effect, as when she is acting Madame Poinçon ('No, no, dear, no . . . Not for the world, not for the world') (Ch. 1); but more often it seems artless as when she says to herself 'Everyday—things with us would mean the greatest things' (Ch. 3). Such an 'open' style of speaking is of course mercilessly revealing. The following extract is certainly childlike in its egocentricity emphasized by the multiplication of first-personal pronouns:

I should learn to see the truth by the same light as great men have seen it by. And then I should know what to do, when I got older; I should see how it was possible to lead a grand life here—now—in England. I don't feel sure about doing good in any way now: everything seems like going on a mission to a people whose language I don't know. (Ch. 3)

The imagery of the last sentence is also typical of Dorothea's speech in these introductory chapters: her analogies are spirited and imaginative, but at the same time, quite explicit. This is no subtle metaphorical thinker. And that we are right in thus emphasizing Dorothea's extreme simplicity is confirmed by the stage direction 'simply' that George Eliot often adds. Does Dorothea's speech alter once she is the wife of Casaubon?

George Eliot makes it clear that Dorothea has often during her marriage to suppress this natural, simple idiom. Her instinctive desire to have her own opinions and projects affirmed by her husband is so often disappointed that she gives up anticipating positive answers from him. Her questions become hesitant and even timid: 'May I talk to you a little instead?' (Ch. 37) and 'May I come out to you in the garden presently?' (Ch. 48). And George Eliot herself speaks of Dorothea's relief in

pouring forth her feelings unchecked: an experience once habitual with her, but hardly ever present since her marriage, which had been a perpetual struggle of energy with fear. (Ch. 39)

However, her tragedy goes deeper than this and to appreciate it we have to know more of the quality of her natural idiom and the personality it reveals.

What are the elements basic to Dorothea when she is being 'herself'? It will be helpful to look at the 'unchecked' conversation with her uncle when she tries to persuade him to make improvements on his estate. She broaches the subject with 'characteristic directness':

'Sir James has been telling me that he is in hope of seeing a great change made soon in your management of the estate—that you are thinking of having the farms valued, and repairs made, and the cottages improved, so that Tipton may look quite another place. Oh, how happy!'—she went on, clasping her hands, with a return to that more childlike impetuous manner which had been subdued since her marriage. 'If I were at home still, I should take to riding again, that I might go about with you and see all that! And you are going to engage Mr Garth, who praised my cottages, Sir James says.'

'Chettam is a little hasty, my dear,' said Mr Brooke, colouring slightly. 'A little hasty, you know. I never said I should do anything of the kind. I never said I should *not* do it, you know.'

'He only feels confident that you will do it', said Dorothea, in a voice as clear and unhesitating as that of a young chorister chanting a *credo*, 'because you mean to enter Parliament as a member who cares for the improvement of the people, and one of the first things to be made better is the state of the land and the labourers. Think of Kit Downes, Uncle, who lives with his wife and seven children in a house with one sitting-room and one bedroom hardly larger than this table! And those poor Dagleys, in their tumbledown farmhouse, where they live in the back kitchen and leave the other rooms to the rats! That is one reason why I did not like the pictures here, dear uncle—which you think me so stupid about. I used to come from the village with all that dirt and coarse ugliness like a pain within me, and the simpering pictures in the drawing-room seemed to me like a wicked attempt to find delight in what is false, while we don't mind how hard the truth is for the neighbours outside our walls. I think we have no right to come forward and urge wider changes for good, until we have tried to alter the evils which lie under our own hands.' (Ch. 39)

There is energy in the exclamatory style through this passage. There is the graphic quality of her analogies—'bedroom hardly larger than this table', there is her unselfconsciousness, absorbed as she is in her 'credo' and the firmness of her rejoinder expressed either in the imperative—'Think of Kit Downes' or the assertion 'we have no right to come forward and urge wider changes for good, until we have tried to alter the evils which lie under our own hands'. 'Ardent' is the word that George Eliot uses for Dorothea and her usage is, as always, precise. How far does Dorothea retain this ardour?

It is with Ladislaw that she is most often her natural self. Apart from moments of embarrassment, this is how she speaks to Will:

'And that will make it all the more honourable,' said Dorothea, ardently. 'Besides, you have so many talents. I have heard from my uncle how well you speak in public, so that everyone is sorry when you leave off, and how clearly you can explain things. And you care that justice should be done to everyone. I am so glad. When we were in Rome, I thought you only cared for poetry and art, and the things that adorn life for those of us who are well off. But now I know you think about the rest of the world.' While she was speaking Dorothea had lost her personal embarrassment and had become like her former self. (Ch. 54)

The speech differs from the example previously given in being simpler, but it still has the affirming emphatic ring ('And that will make it all the more honourable'). The prompting tone of 'And you care that justice should be done to everyone' and the universal 'everyone' and 'the rest of the world' are characteristically energetic. Whatever may be Ladislaw's faults, there is something in him that allows Dorothea to retain her ardour.

Other stylistic correlatives to her ardour which persist till the end are her forceful imperatives, her strong diction and her use of intensifying adverbs. There is an urgency and force of utterance in Dorothea that we find in no other speaker in *Middlemarch*. Her imperatives are often passionate entreaties 'Forgive me! . . .' (Ch. 21), she says to Casaubon, and to Ladislaw, 'Promise me that you will not again, to anyone, speak of that subject' (Ch. 22). She develops her own elliptical way of commanding compassion, '—please not to mention that again' (Ch. 37), she says to Lydgate. She continues to use words possessing the utmost force—'It is wicked to let people think evil of anyone falsely, when it can be hindered' (Ch. 76). Finally there is her persistent use of intensifiers: She is 'very grateful' to Mr Casaubon for loving her (Ch. 5). She is 'very glad' to hear from Ladislaw that she is a poem (Ch. 22). She has 'very little to do', and wishes 'very much' to see Lydgate to help him (Ch. 76).

Dorothea's most emphatic resource of all is her disarming

directness. The overwhelming majority of her sentences have as their subject the personal pronoun, 'I'. To Ladislaw at the very end of the novel, she cries characteristically: 'Oh, I cannot bear it—my heart will break . . . I don't mind about poverty—I hate my wealth . . . We could live quite well on my own fortune—it is too much—seven hundred a year—I want so little—no new clothes—and I will learn what everything costs' (Ch. 83). *Middlemarch* presents us with several studies in egoism. Egoism, a study of Dorothea's speech would seem to suggest, is not simply a matter of having an 'I' any more than altruism is a matter of losing it.

Also retained, but perhaps less wholly sympathetic, is Dorothea's simplicity with its ambiguous element of 'childlike' egoism. For instance, after her husband's death she says:

'I should like to take a great deal of land and drain it and make a little colony, where everybody should work, and all the work should be done well. I should know every one of the people and be their friend. I am going to have great consultations with Mr Garth: he can tell me almost everything I want to know.' (Ch. 55)

George Eliot makes no comment but her ironic response to these Utopian dreams is expressed in the 'great deal of land' which to satisfy Dorothea will need '*draining*' (just as Milton needed to be blind) before she could render her not unobtrusive services. The colony will be cosily 'little' but Dorothea's universal 'everybody', 'every one', 'everything' will make it a whole world where she will be befriended because of what she has done. This is fantasy, the sort of opiate which George Eliot would always reject.[19] Unless we attend carefully to the implications of the style, we shall, like F. R. Leavis, miss the criticism which persists in George Eliot's attitude to her heroine. Dorothea does not become perfect, the irony focused on her does not altogether disappear.

One element in her ardour which Dorothea does lose permanently and as a result of the whole stultifying environment of Middlemarch is her imaginative use of analogy. In the introductory chapters of the novel, Dorothea had likened the blonde-haired, red-whiskered Sir James Chettam to 'a *cochon de lait*'

(Ch. 2) and, on another occasion she 'feels scourged' (Ch. 4). Later, talking to Ladislaw in Rome about her response to art Dorothea says: 'At first when I enter a room where the walls are covered with frescoes, or with rare pictures, I feel a kind of awe—like a child present at great ceremonies where there are grand robes and processions; . . . It is painful to be told that everything is very fine and not to be able to feel that it is fine— something like being blind, while people talk of the sky' (Ch. 21). She develops her explanation a little later:

'The painting and sculpture may be wonderful, but the feeling is often low and brutal, and sometimes even ridiculous. Here and there I see what takes me at once as noble—something that I might compare with the Alban Mountains or the sunset from the Pincian Hill. . . .' (Ch. 22)

Finally, she describes her belief to Ladislaw:

'That by desiring what is perfectly good, even when we don't quite know what it is and cannot do what we would, we are part of the divine power against evil—widening the skirts of light and making the struggles with darkness narrower.' (Ch. 39)

Apart from the examples given above (see page 75) where Dorothea uses analogies in the moment of recovering her old spirit, and apart from talking to Rosamond about 'murdering' marriage, these are the only examples of figurative expression I can find spoken by Dorothea after her marriage to Casaubon. It is, I think, highly significant that they are all spoken to Ladislaw. But it is also true that they are all taken from the first half of *Middlemarch*, and that Dorothea does not enter marriage with Ladislaw with graphic phrases on her lips.

This would seem to be an instance of a characteristic of Dorothea's speech that is shown to atrophy. The heroine, on the evidence of the above account, would appear to have lost her facility in the use of a rich linguistic resource. Dorothea will never again illustrate her views with reference to 'scourges', 'sunsets', 'processions', of even *cochons de lait*.

Dorothea's other sad loss, mirrored in her speech, is her confidence that people will say 'yes' to her. In all her early questions she prompts corroboration by using negatives, 'Will you not now do . . .' 'Will you not make up your mind . . .'

(Ch. 20). But she has difficulty in eliciting from Casaubon the positive response she desires. She then turns to others, hoping that they may be positive about Casaubon. Thus she says to Ladislaw, '. . . it seems to me that with Mr Casaubon's learning he must have before him the same materials as German scholars —has he not?' (Ch. 22). And to Lydgate, when her husband is ill, 'But Mr Casaubon will soon be here again, I hope. Is he not making progress?' (Ch. 30). Eventually, to many people, her questions become purely rhetorical. 'What do we live for, if it is not to make life less difficult to each other?' (Ch. 72).

Dorothea's rhetorical questions are a moving dramatization of someone dangerously isolated, affirming her values out loud in an effort to keep a grip on them. This accounts too for much of her hyperbole. She recognizes this habit of 'speaking too strongly' (Ch. 62). Twice only in the latter half of *Middlemarch* does Dorothea make a desperate effort to regain affirmation and in each case it is on behalf of somebody else. Thus she meets Rosamond's 'polite impassibility' (Ch. 81) with 'cordial pleading tones'.

'You will not think me too troublesome, when I tell you that I came to talk to you about the injustice that has been shown towards Mr Lydgate. It will cheer you—will it not?—to know a great deal about him, that he may not like to speak about himself just because it is in his own vindication and to his own honour. You will like to know that your husband has warm friends, who have not left off believing in his high character? You will let me speak of this without thinking that I take a liberty?' (Ch. 81)

On this occasion Dorothea evokes a response. It is her major triumph that, with all the discouragement her ardour meets with, she still does urge affirmation. We know the triumph, because it is uniquely successful. On the only other occasion after the death of her husband that she dares seek support for her generous impulses, she is repulsed. It is when Farebrother has said that there is no proof for Lydgate's innocence. Dorothea exclaims: 'Oh, how cruel! . . . And would you not like to be the one person who believed in that man's innocence, if the rest of the world belied him?' (Ch. 72). Dorothea does not get the positive answer her ardour demands.

Disappointed in this hope, Dorothea falls back on people's readiness to say 'no'. Her 'way', we are told, is still 'ardent' (Ch. 62) but the form of the question is different. To Ladislaw she says, 'Do you suppose that I ever disbelieved in you?' (Ch. 62). And, later in the scene referred to above in which she is talking to Farebrother, she says 'energetically', 'You don't believe that Mr Lydgate is guilty of anything base?' (Ch. 71).

To ask questions in this way the key words have to be negative; Dorothea has to bring herself to utter words like 'guilty' and 'disbelieved' whereas we feel the natural tendency of 'a young chorister chanting a *credo*' would be more positive.

To sum up, Dorothea's tragedy is that life in Middlemarch denies her public expression—either in words or in acts—of her ardour. She does not lose her 'essential nature'. Her sense of identity remains—she is still direct and her emphases have not weakened. Yet her ardent soul is all but muted. There is loss of 'individuality'.[20] She no longer expresses herself figuratively, no longer looks for affirmation. Only with her future husband will she sometimes indulge the parallelisms of rhetoric, once so precious to her. To all others, passion can no longer be adequately represented in words. At the beginning of the book Dorothea had declared to Celia: 'It is offensive to me to say that Sir James could think I was fond of him. Besides, it is not the right word for the feeling I must have towards the man I would accept as a husband' (Ch. 4). Three years later, at the end of the novel, the two sisters talk to each other again. Celia asks Dorothea about Ladislaw: 'Is he very fond of you, Dodo?' and Dorothea replies: 'I hope so. I am very fond of him' (Ch. 84). Dorothea's essential nature has deepened in its capacity for feeling, but she has had to submit to a conventional and inadequate expression of her love. The meaning of the book is nowhere more clear than here as we analyse the very words Dorothea uses. Her changing style *is* her changing self, and George Eliot allows it to speak for herself. She never tells us explicitly in what Dorothea's 'Sad sacrifice' consists—it is for us to hear the grass grow.

If George Eliot has this skill in characterization through individual speech, why then does she do so much of the work

herself? Why is the inward reflection of her characters not presented in a brilliantly animated and individualized interior
monologue? Is this at least not an artistic fault which we must
regret—the sort of clumsy, uncoordinated fumbling we might
expect from that 'osseous lengthy countenance' David Cecil
discovers in the author's portrait? Or is there perhaps a good
reason behind George Eliot's chosen method of presenting the
inner life of her characters? I believe that there is.

In the treatment of her characters' thought, George Eliot has
developed a technique which allows her to give both an internal
and an external account of their experience. It is yet another
example of the way in which George Eliot makes her point by
zig-zagging. We oscillate between an emotional identification
with a character and an obliquely judicious response to their
situation.

The way in which George Eliot achieves this effect is princi-
pally by using what is called *erlebte Rede*. Professor Quirk has
pointed out that English has 'no generally acknowledged term'
for this device.[21] In French it is known as *le style indirect libre*.[22]
It is a form of exposition readily available in German (which
may be where George Eliot first became familiar with it), it
approaches the immediacy of *oratio recta* whilst retaining the
grammatical form of *oratio obliqua*. Thus, describing Dorothea's
reaction to finding Ladislaw with Rosamond, George Eliot
writes:

The fire of Dorothea's anger was not easily spent, and it flamed out in
fitful returns of spurning reproach. Why had he come obtruding his
life into hers, hers that might have been whole enough without him?
Why had he brought his cheap regard and his lip born words to her
who had nothing paltry to give in exchange? He knew that he was
deluding her—wished, in the very moment of farewell, to make her
believe that he gave her the whole price of her heart, and knew that he
had spent it half before. Why had he not stayed among the crowd of
whom she asked nothing—but only prayed that they might be less
contemptible? (Ch. 80)

The first sentence of this extract is straightforward author
narrative. But then, without any warning, the reader is presented
with a dramatization of the 'spurning reproach'. It is not of

course pure dialogue that we hear: the verbs and pronouns are those of indirect speech. But indirect speech, made subordinate to an author's 'dixit', would have had much less immediacy of impact than is achieved by the use of the free indirect style. The questions are preserved as questions instead of being turned into the quasi-statement—'she asked why he had come . . .' George Eliot's form of speech reporting retains much more of the colloquial original.

Lisa Glauser,[23] as far as I am aware, was the first critic to notice the use of *erlebte Rede* in George Eliot's novels. She talks of George Eliot's passionate love of truth scrutinizing both character and motive; her people, she says, are seen from the inside, her novels exciting dramas of moral conflict. She goes on to speak of the intuitive inward looking and passionate personal life of the characters presented to us. She points out what a useful correlative *erlebte Rede* is to such a view. By it, George Eliot can achieve effects like the following in Chapter 81.

She was beginning to fear that she should not be able to suppress herself enough to the end of this meeting, and while her hand was still resting on Rosamond's lap, though the hand underneath it was withdrawn, she was struggling against her own rising sobs. She tried to master herself with the thought that this might be a turning-point in three lives—not in her own; no, there the irrevocable had happened, but—in those three lives which were touching her with the solemn neighbourhood of danger and distress. The fragile creature who was crying close by her—there might still be time to rescue her from the misery of false incompatible bonds; and this moment was unlike any other: she and Rosamond could never be together again with the same thrilling consciousness of yesterday within them both. (Ch. 81)

Glauser gives this and many other examples from *Middlemarch* of the way in which, through *erlebte Rede*, we are taken into the minds of the characters. Writing on Flaubert's use of the same technique, Stephen Ullman points out[24] that anguish finds its natural expression in this medium. But Ullman stresses the impersonality of the device and talks about the 'author's disappearance behind his characters',[25] as though what we were left with was just 'anguish'. He quotes Flaubert's famous dictum, 'L'auteur, dans son oeuvre, doit être comme Dieu dans l'univers, présent partout et visible nulle part', and comments, 'Free indirect style is the exact equivalent, on the linguistic plane, of this withdrawal of the author from his work.'[26]

Yet it might be supposed that pure dialogue was a more exact equivalent of this withdrawal. Leo Spitzer's description of *erlebte Rede* as 'pseudo-objective' would seem more appropriate. He accepts that what *erlebte Rede* presents us with is the subjective voices of the characters but adds they are meant to count as pseudo-objective presentation by the author. This surely is what we have in George Eliot—a balance between the inside and the outside point of view.

This seems to me the important achievement of the technique in the hands of George Eliot. The thoughts we hear do not come to us voiced in the actual idiom of the characters themselves. Translated into *oratio recta* they would sound slightly strange on the lips of their owners. It is partly a matter of decorum: in the first example given above, Dorothea could not herself say, 'Why did he not stay among the crowd of whom I ask nothing —but only pray that they might be less contemptible?' Partly it is a matter of tense, syntax and diction—Dorothea could not be responsible for the 'preconceived' of the following:

The clear heights where she expected to walk in full communion had become difficult to see even in her imagination: the delicious repose of the soul on a complete superior had been shaken into uneasy effort and alarmed with dim presentiment. When would the days begin of that active wifely devotion which was to strengthen her husband's life and exalt her own? Never perhaps, as she had preconceived them: but somehow—still somehow. (Ch. 78)

The voice we hear has been distanced by *erlebte Rede*: the very presentation in this way is an implicit invitation to consider what is being said. George Eliot indicates that what we are hearing is a dramatic statement. She does not fully dramatize for fear perhaps that we would get carried away by the rhetoric of her character. 'This is the sort of way this character would represent it' is the effective message we get from the author.

In her survey of the novel, Lisa Glauser can find no use of *erlebte Rede* to express the central ideas of the novelists of the eighteenth and early nineteenth centuries. Only after the period of revolutionary romanticism was interest aroused in the inner life . . . 'but there was still lacking the balance, the distance, the muting which is the other premise of *erlebte Rede*'. She continues: 'In George Eliot's novels we find for the first time all the conditions fulfilled for its complete development as the highly modern technique of expression we know.'[27] To the qualities she discerns in this technique which I have already noted, the intuitive inward-looking element, she adds the 'other premise'— critical analysis. It is one more piece of evidence of George Eliot's two preoccupations in *Middlemarch*—the problem of the expression of the inner life and the problem of how to evaluate its quality from the outside—an outside that can never be wholly objective. It is even possible that it is this choice of the technique of *erlebte Rede* as opposed to straight dramatized reflection or interior monologue, which saves George Eliot and the reader from the trap of becoming uncritically identified with Dorothea's thoughts—a trap which Henry James for instance did not escape in his presentation of Maggie Verver. In other words *erlebte Rede* is yet one more variation on George Eliot's stylistic aim of combining emotional involvement and ironic criticism. She achieves this through her 'own' voice, through Dorothea's speech mannerisms, and finally through this oblique yet sympathetic presentation of Dorothea's thoughts.

There are, I think, two major criticisms to be made of the kind of stylistic analysis I have attempted here. The first is that it must necessarily select, and hence distort, even more than interpretative, deductive criticism does. Then, it is often said that no reader, however serious, can possibly by aware of all or even any of these detailed stylistic points dissected by the linguist, and that in fact too developed an awareness of these stylistic *minutiae* would even run counter to the overwhelming impression made by the work as a whole.

To the first argument I would reply generally that though I have selected examples of dramatic ventriloquism I am not claiming that *Middlemarch* is *all* dramatic ventriloquism. Of course we can all find scattered through the novel many passages in which we feel that the narrator is not rôle-playing, but taking

84

direct responsibility for her statements. I claim merely that dramatic ventriloquism is an important aspect of her style, and one that has been largely overlooked.

Then, to the argument that the reader is not conscious of style, I would reply that he must be *unconsciously* responding to the succession of stylistic stimuli provided by the author. That he remains unconscious of them in *Middlemarch* is owing to George Eliot's emphasis on realism. George Eliot has not composed from a palette of bright colours; nor, with her quiet colours, has she achieved sharp, startling distinctions of 'gradient'.[28] Her gradations are subtle. Finally, to the argument that the linguist necessarily misses the wood for the trees, I would say with Leo Spitzer: 'the lifeblood of the poetic creation is everywhere the same, whether we tap the organism at "language" or "ideas", at "plot" or at "composition".'[29] What I and other students of George Eliot's style have seen, *is there*; the ironic, ever-shifting, multiple points of view from which Dorothea is seen, her subtly individual speech rhythms and vocabulary which change ever so slightly to mirror her gain in humanity and her loss of confidence in its expression—these *are there*, and when we have once seen them, we can never again speak of George Eliot's style as often not 'felicitous', because ponderous, crudely didactic, or unable to achieve its intended effects. What George Eliot is saying in *Middlemarch*, she could have said in no other way. It is impossible to maintain that 'We like what she says, but not how she says it.' If we think the ideas could have been better served, this is because the ideas are ours and not the author's.

Thus the main justification for stylistic analysis lies in my opinion in its inductive approach. This means that the linguistic critic must start from a self-effacing surrender to the text as he first observes the peculiarities of his author's language, then notes its effects and finally forms some hypothesis concerning the appropriateness of the means to the end. As Spitzer says, finally we will make 'the return trip to all the other groups of observations in order to find whether the "inward form" one has tentatively constructed gives an account of the whole'.[30] It was Ruskin, as far as I know, who was the first critic to insist upon the importance of 'annihilating our own personality' if we are to enter another's,—that of 'your author'.[31] More recently, Michael Riffaterre, in an essay on stylistic analysis, has pointed out the way in which an author relies upon his style to limit the reader's 'freedom of perception in the process of decoding', 'the only procedure open to the encoder, when he wants to impose his own interpretation on his poem, is thus to prevent the reader from inferring or predicting any important feature. For predictability may result in superficial reading: unpredictability will compel attention.'[32]

The principal aim of this essay has been to modify the commonly accepted notion of the clumsy predictability of George Eliot's style in *Middlemarch* and in so doing, to deepen our understanding of Dorothea.

The Language of the Novel
Imagery

HILDA M. HULME

ON 24 OCTOBER 1871 George Eliot's publisher, John Black-wood, had his day's work destroyed by a visit from Alexander Main, a rhapsodic admirer of her novels ('the Gusher' as he was privately called), who was seeking permission to prepare a volume of extracts from George Eliot's writings.[1] Blackwood describes with some enjoyment his talk with the 'little fellow': 'He is quite an enthusiast and told me he did "not read much but he read deep". He worships George Eliot as having done for the Novel what Shakespeare did for the Drama. When he wound up some glowing period by saying she was "Concrete" I was nearly upset.'[2]

The visiting linguist who seeks to examine some of the detail of the *Middlemarch* imagery in an attempt to discover whence this imagery derives its characteristic force cannot but feel certain affinities with Blackwood's guest, one who had 'evidently seen nothing of the world or scarcely' and who 'used his knife in a dangerous manner at lunch'. Such an examination is necessarily experimental and there is difficulty at the outset in defining one's aim while yet preserving freedom of action. To express it in the most general terms, one would like to find out, from sources outside the novel, what kinds of imagery (perhaps also what ideas about imagery) the novelist has at her disposal and at the same time to see how, within the novel, she adapts this image-language to the purposes of her art. Supposing that such an investigation could be carried out systematically and at full scale, it would be hard, we may agree, for even the most disciplined of critics to fit together into a satisfactory sequence the resulting patchwork collection of accumulated material and I shall not therefore pretend to any very logical order of exposition when describing, within the limits of a single chapter, the several different approaches to this problem which have appeared to me of interest. It seems best also not to take up space with any attempt at a composite definition of the term 'image', although I hope that sufficient examples are offered to make quite clear what kind of 'imagery' I am talking about in the different sections.

It may be convenient first to mention two quite considerable difficulties which have to be taken into account throughout. The would-be commentator is only too well aware that any image taken from the *Middlemarch* context loses some of its subtlety of reference and, what is worse, acquires a hardness of outline which stands out over-clearly against the general background of the writer's style and purpose; further, the meaning of an image, even within its context, is not static; its value is different for different readers. First, that is to say, the very act of selection is bound to involve a kind of falsification; any knife is used dangerously on work where 'nothing is superfluous, but all is in organic dependence, nothing is there for detached effect, but the whole is effect'.[3] These are Lewes's words (1855) on the 'perfect unity of impression' produced upon the reader by Goethe's *Iphigenia*, but George Eliot's own ideal as suggested in one of her earliest articles (1847) is very similar. Watching in a Paris studio the progress of a noble picture, the moralizing essayist (comparing life and art) loves to think how 'the perfect whole exists in the imagination of the artist, before his pencil has marked the canvass,—to observe how every minute stroke, every dismal-looking layer of colour, conduces to the ultimate effect, and how completely the creative genius which has conceived the result can calculate the necessary means'.[4] Twenty-four years later, during the writing of *Middlemarch* (while it was yet 'too early for such definite arrangements' as to where to make the break between Parts I and II of the novel), she explains to Blackwood 'I don't see how I can leave anything out, because I hope there is nothing that will be seen to be irrelevant to my design.'[5] When a long novel is so intricately planned, the 'necessary means' so deliberately and finely calculated, much of its minor imagery is necessarily unmarked and underemphasized. It is left, apparently, to make its own effects, and perhaps it were well, to adapt Casaubon's idiom, that it should be so left. For the 'meaning' of even the minor image is not fixed and determinable; its range of reference changes as the reader gives attention to this or that inter-relation within the novel's whole design. Jerome Beaty has shown that for George Eliot herself the writing of *Middlemarch* was 'a process of evolution and of discovery',[6] and it may well be argued that the individual reader has similarly to make his own discoveries, his view of the novel's language changing and developing as he reads. He too, it has been suggested, may prefer to 'keep the germinating grain away from the light'. One must recognize, at all events, that the interrupting commentator who selects a single image for particular examination gives that image at once an inartistic over-importance. The evolving relationship of reader and author is broken, and an outsider's exposition may well seem arbitrary, laborious, incomplete, or over-elaborate. To take one example: when Casaubon, the expected dinner-guest, is 'already an accepted lover' and Celia, in George Eliot's wonderfully extended progressiveness of tense, is feeling 'a sort of shame mingled with a sense of the ludicrous' at her own suspicion that Dodo might really be 'bordering on such an extravagance' of mind that 'could tend towards such an issue', she observes how during the afternoon 'Dorothea, instead of settling down with her usual diligent interest to some occupation, simply leaned her elbow on an open book, and looked out of the window' (Ch. 5). The author's later manuscript addition here, 'at the great cedar silvered with the damp', as well as being an accurately observed pictorial detail, might seem perhaps, at a third or fourth re-reading of the novel, an added marginal reference to Dorothea's emotional position.[7] She might, so to say, be looking out from her old life at a new opportunity; certainly she thinks of Casaubon with proud and reverential awe, and 'cedar' has obvious Biblical connotations; 'silvered' then would express the idealism of 'where your husband was a sort of father' (Ch. 1), its static beauty undiminished by her uncle's earlier warning, perhaps now recalled to the reader's consciousness, that 'every year will tell upon him' (Ch. 4). 'Damp' we find later as a Casaubon quality; it could here carry us forward to Celia's unspoken feeling (when Dorothea has returned from her wedding journey), her regarding of 'Mr Casaubon's learning as a kind of damp which might in due time saturate a neighbouring body' (Ch. 28). It would, no doubt, be reading a little too deep to suppose from Dorothea's simply leaning her elbow on an open book, in this 'damp' context, that she shares a little ('beforehand, you know') in her sister's notion that learning may come from physical contact. Yet in a novel where physical posture and physical movement so often represent mental state and emotional change, it is hard to know what limits the author would have us set to our readiness in picking up such significances. Even the simple 'leaning' action accumulates contextual reference as the story continues. Should it be that in resting some of her weight on the open book, Dorothea has some half-conscious hope of leaning a little on her husband's openness of intellect, this hope is ended even before Celia comes to visit her on her return from her wedding-journey: already 'the delicious repose of the soul on a complete superior had been shaken into uneasy effort and alarmed with dim presentiment' (Ch. 28). It is Dorothea who, not long afterwards, supports Mr Casaubon's weight, when he is taken ill in the library (Ch. 29). This brief example will sufficiently indicate the dangers of attempting an over-clear analysis of image-'meaning'; there are no rules of procedure which lay down how strong a lens we should apply to such finely-wrought linguistic structures, and it is all too easy to 'find ourselves making interpretations' which, lacking George Eliot's subtle and spacious ordering, 'turn out to be rather coarse'.

A CHARACTERISTIC 'MOVEMENT' IMAGE

Many of George Eliot's readers would agree, I think, that Main's term 'Concrete' by which Blackwood's composure was nearly upset seems, now as then, precisely and totally appropriate. It has an obvious relation to the larger purposes of the novelist's art, the embodiment of general truth in a particular narrative example, and is probably also the best of single words to describe that quality on which Edith Simcox comments in an early review of *Middlemarch* (1 January 1873)—the author's gift, 'shared only, amongst contemporaries by Mr Browning, of choosing similes and illustrations, that do really illustrate the nature of the things compared'.[8] Particularly striking to the present-day observer is her ability to select and control an accurate kinaesthetic imagery, through which, in a novel-world where little is static but the furniture, the reader's whole attention can be concentrated, for a few words' space, on just that emotional energy, narrowly limited and fully charged, which 'moves' or holds the novel-character. This kind of imagery is indeed so often and so effortlessly employed that, if we measure by George Eliot's standards, there is nothing remarkable in the following example, which tells of how Lydgate, after dining at Mr Vincy's and for the first time enjoying Rosamond's music, went home 'and read far into the smallest hour', bringing to a new book on fever 'a much more testing vision of details and relations . . . than he had ever thought it necessary to apply to the complexities of love and marriage' (Ch. 16).

As he threw down his book, stretched his legs towards the embers in the grate, and clasped his hands at the back of his head, in that agreeable after-glow of excitement when thought lapses from examination of a specific object into a suffusive sense of its connections with all the rest of our existence—seems, as it were, to throw itself on its back after vigorous swimming and float with the repose of unexhausted strength—Lydgate felt a triumphal delight in his studies, and something like pity for those less lucky men who were not of his profession.

It is easy to see that this one sentence contains a three-fold series of coincident movement patterns: there is first the account of Lydgate's actual physical movement; then the change in the process of mental activity which is necessarily set out in abstract terms (mainly abstract nouns) and thirdly the imagined physical movement of swimmer turning floater. Through the simply organized interconnection of these three kinds of movement, abstract is made concrete and the double unity of body and mind, thinker and thought, is readily established. Lydgate the thinker changes his posture as he rests from reading; the swimmer, which is his thought, and which has been occupied in examining a specific object—driving forward, that is to say, in a given direction—changes its posture also, throwing itself on its back as Lydgate throws down his book. And as Lydgate lies back in his chair, his thought also 'lapses', the unexhausted thought-swimmer stretching out its body in the water, with its hands, no doubt, clasped at the back of its head in Lydgate's easy attitude. The language-base on which George Eliot has constructed the swimming-floating thought image is a part of ordinary speech; when work goes 'swimmingly' we all know what it is to feel 'buoyed up' with confidence. The 'as it were' phrase, we may notice, which introduces the image, is there not because the writer is working with an unusual image range, but so that she may carry the sentence more easily over the necessary pronoun changes; his book, our existence, to throw itself. And it is a true observation also, as all swimmers know, that in the effortless floating motion, as one looks up into 'illuminated space' (the 'inward light' of Lydgate's earlier 'fever' thoughts), consciousness of an urgent separate identity is lessened; there is the sense instead of belonging to an older, more instinctive, liquid world: 'thought lapses . . . into a suffusive sense of its connections with all the rest of our existence'.[9]

It is interesting to note how the writer's exact economy of presentation enforces the abstract-concrete equivalence. Of Lydgate's three physical actions, 'threw down', 'stretched', 'clasped', only the first verb 'throw' is repeated in the metaphorical movement; it is left to the reader to complete the series. The only properties in the actual physical scene are Lydgate's book, which is discarded, and the 'embers in the grate'; there is not, for example, a chair in which he may lie back until my commentary provides it; all that the narrator requires him to have are what the reader is to supply for the swimmer, 'legs', 'hands' and the 'back of his head'. And even though the time is 'far into the smallest hour', no such adjective as 'dying' diminishes the embers; Lydgate's awareness of their agreeable glow after he finishes his reading is parallel, no doubt, to 'that agreeable after-glow of excitement' which follows vigorous thought and 'vigorous swimming'. As the reader, so to say, supplies the missing parts of such descriptions, he enters to some extent into the thoughts and feelings which are described. In this particular instance however we can see also that the novelist has quite deliberately set a limit to reader-character identification. Although Lydgate's existence becomes 'our' existence as thought takes on the 'sense of its connections with all the rest' of life, *we* are not grammatically present in the 'vigorous swimming'. It is clear, if we think about it, that the superlative energy of 'unexhausted strength' can belong only to part of our lives; for the rest of our existence we take our place with 'those less lucky men' (the Farebrothers of this world) for whom the vigorous swimmer feels 'something like pity'.

The placing of this incident within the narrative and the setting together of other swimming-floating images in the Lydgate context bring further correspondences and less clear cross-relations into the reader's own less active thought. Lydgate's throwing himself on his back after vigorous swimming to float with the repose of unexhausted strength seems, as a single unbroken movement, essentially a masculine and a sexual image; if, at the same time, the image is seen as two contrasted movements, such a contrast has an obvious relevance to the career-marriage opposition which is to break his intellectual strength. The reader has been warned in the previous chapter that 'that distinction of mind which belonged to his intellectual ardour did not penetrate his feeling and judgment about furniture or women'. Miss Brooke he has earlier found 'a little too earnest' (Ch. 10). 'The society of such women was about as relaxing as going from your work to teach the second form, instead of reclining in a paradise.' Yet although Lydgate had quite soon been conscious of being fascinated by Miss Vincy, 'he did not in the least suppose that he had lost his balance and fallen in love' (Ch. 11). At twenty-seven and with eight hundred pounds left him after buying his practice he was, we are told, 'at a starting point which makes many a man's career a fine subject for betting' if one could appreciate 'all the niceties of inward balance, by which a man swims and makes his point or else is carried headlong' (Ch. 15). Lydgate's first intention was to swim. As he walked home from Mr Vincy's on this particular night he thought 'of Rosamond and her music only in the second place; and though, when her turn came, he dwelt on the image of her for the rest of his walk, he . . . had no sense that any new current had set into his life'.

The verb 'dwelt on' here which follows more energetic thoughts of Mr Bulstrode and the new hospital, echoes back a little to the 'reclining in a paradise' which is Lydgate's idea of relaxing after his work; it leads on also to the repose which is to be enjoyed when the book is thrown down. The agreeableness of floating is mentioned once more before Lydgate's day closes. After his reading is finished and he thinks with satisfaction of how his profession calls forth 'the highest intellectual strain' (vigorous swimming) and yet keeps him in 'good warm contact' (embers, after-glow) with his neighbours, the thought of Mr Farebrother 'brought back the Vincys and all the pictures of the evening. They floated in his mind agreeably enough.' The intricacy of the image relations forbids more detailed comment; it is clear, at least, that the particular repetition on which attention has been concentrated is very delicately handled. Some sense of it still lingers perhaps towards the end of the story, when Lydgate hears from Dorothea 'the first assurance of belief in him' and gives himself up, 'for the first time in his life, to the exquisite sense of leaning entirely on a generous sympathy, without any check of proud reserve' (Ch. 76). And it is interesting here to see with what care and intuition the writer is selecting her image-language: 'leaning' is a manuscript correction for an earlier 'throwing himself'. It seems indeed that the more vigorous action is now out of context. As Lydgate says of his time in Middlemarch, 'I had some ambition . . . I thought I had more strength and mastery . . . I have lost all spirit about carrying on my life here.'

IMAGERY FROM EVERYDAY LANGUAGE

Main's extensive admiration of George Eliot 'as having done for the Novel what Shakespeare did for the Drama' finds some echo in our present-day enthusiasm for her work; it is not without reason that we are reproached, as a modern critic has said, for thinking that every novel would be *Middlemarch* if it could. And even if we leave out of consideration what is perhaps her major 'Shakespearean' characteristic, her use of the larger image as part of the novel structure, so that relations are set up 'independently of the time-sequence which is the story',[10] certain features of her minor language, her handling of the cliché-image and her play on general linguistic expectancies have something also of the Shakespearean power to surprise, the once-only liveliness of his dramatic dialogue. The language that Shakespeare made is deeply rooted in the language that he found. George Eliot also in her minor imagery draws largely on the diction of common life, often using 'with a difference' the cliché-images of everyday language, so that a certain tension is established between generalized and individual expression. When, on occasion, the stock images appear in their ordinary form, one may deduce that the novelist is using them of deliberate intent, so as to show the 'mental flavour' of the speaker. John Raffles speaking to Mr Rigg Featherstone, 'without humbug' as he claims, uses cliché after cliché in a palpably insincere appeal which combines whining sentimentality with the pretence of shrewd self-interest. His mental flavour, we are told, 'seemed to have a stale odour of travellers' rooms in the commercial hotels of that period' (Ch. 41). Fred Vincy's mental flavour is that of the rather sulky schoolboy when he speaks to Mary of his 'dreadful certainty' that he will 'be bowled out by Farebrother'; he feels 'horribly jealous' and speaks in a 'piqued tone' with 'some rage' and irritation; he 'can have no fair chance' (Ch. 57). The cricketing image is repeated when Mr Farebrother sits down by Mary at the Vincy's New Year party, and Fred's enjoyment is 'streaked with jealousy'. He 'used to be much more easy about his own accomplishments in the days when he had not begun to dread being "bowled out by Farebrother", and this terror was still before him' (Ch. 63). This quotation from Fred's past shows something of his progress in self-knowledge but the mental flavour remains the same: life is still seen rather as a game which sportsmen play according to the rules, and a young man's cricket may be expected to improve. Fred's terror has in it no morbid self-depreciation; it is based rather on a sturdy self-interest and a friendly acceptance of his own potential.

There are many ways in which the collective experience which underlies the cliché image may be brought into play in the novel language. Sometimes, as Shakespeare so often does, George Eliot offers an old image in a new form. It seems from one or two examples that a quite simple re-phrasing can very effectively imply frustration. When Will pays his farewell visit to Dorothea in Rome and she gently reminds him that Lowick is her chosen home, 'Will did not know what to say, since it would not be useful for him to embrace her slippers, and tell her that he would die for her: it was clear that she required nothing of the sort' (Ch. 22). Will's sense of the non-usefulness of the translated image conveys well enough his realization that all he can change are the forms of language; he can tone down and domesticate the exaggeratedness of the 'kiss her feet' image but not change at all the reality of 'that stone prison at Lowick'. A somewhat similar instance is found after the reply comes from Quallingham to Rosamond's letter, when Rosamond will not admit her 'secret meddling' and her 'false assent', and Lydgate, 'checkmated', asks himself 'What place was there in her mind for a remonstrance to lodge in?' (Ch. 65). Such a variation on the usual phrase 'How to get it into her head?' fairly indicates the speaker's frustrated sense that every 'how' has been tried and that the mind itself has no room in it for what another nature feels in opposition to its own. And although the crudity of the old proverb 'In at one ear and out at the other' has no place in the language which Rosamond and Lydgate use to each other, it may well be present in some degree to the reader's understanding. Earlier in the novel (Ch. 58) some ironic contrast may be implied between the naïve over-refinement of Rosamond's standards and the more general values of a wider, more plainly-spoken world; she suggests to Lydgate that he should talk more at dinner to their guest, his cousin, the baronet's third son. 'You really look so absent sometimes—you seem to be seeing through his head into something behind it, instead of looking at him.' Rosamond speaks as if she had no notion of someone's being 'empty-headed', and as if she had never 'seen through a person', much less 'looked straight through him'.

Many instances could be cited where the re-wording of a usual image allows a new exactness. Language seems to arise from situation, the speaker or narrator finding a new form of expression to fit the individual case. Cadwallader knows well that even if he wished to do so, he cannot influence Brooke to defer Dorothea's marriage: 'Brooke is a very good fellow, but pulpy; he will run into any mould, but he won't keep shape' (Ch. 8). This use of the active 'running into a mould' rather than the more usual passive form, 'being moulded', suggests at once the facile non-gritty compliance of Dorothea's uncle; probably also he is made the active subject of the sentence because, in the end, all would depend on his activity. Ladislaw feels a similar doubt of Mr Brooke's capacity when he is coaching him for his electoral speech (Ch. 51): 'the only way in which Mr Brooke could be coerced into thinking of the right arguments at the right time was to be well plied with them till they took up all the room in his brain. But here there was the difficulty of finding room, so many things having been taken in beforehand.' Unhappily, we are told, the 'pat opening' of Mr Brooke's speech had soon slipped away, as can so easily happen 'when fear clutches us, and a glass of sherry is hurrying like smoke among our ideas'. The author's re-wording here is obviously more telling than the blunted generality of 'fumes of wine going to one's head'. Even where no space is left, the smoke can make its way, and the added visual image blurs the eyes.

Modern linguistic theory has shown, to quote J. R. Firth, that 'a word is known by the company it keeps'; the meaning of the single word can be tightly controlled by verbal context. George Eliot's images are frequently reinforced and extended so that such words and expressions as were once metaphorical but have long since lost much of their figurative force (coming, if I may re-apply her novel metaphors, 'from the very fact of frequency' . . . 'to be shapen after the average and fit to be packed by the gross') have their original energy restored. Occasionally we can see this process in the manuscript changes made by the novelist in her final revision. Dorothea speaks to Will of her desire, even when she was a little girl, 'to help some one who did great works, so that his burthen might be lighter', and Will counters promptly within the same range of imagery 'But you may easily help too much and get over-wrought yourself' (Ch. 37). It seems to me that the 'over-wrought' of his reply is a warning to Dorothea, not from Will only but from generations of earlier speakers, that even metaphorical burdens may have real weight. This way of combining two, as it were, suspended metaphors within a simple physical image George Eliot has to perfection. In this particular instance we may observe in her final draft the result of a further slight re-thinking and re-feeling of the figurative language used; 'carry the help too far' which is substituted for the earlier 'help too much' adds a little to the load-distance physical imagery and so makes clearer the 'burthen'-'over-wrought' connection. Meanwhile however nothing is lost in simplicity of language, and the 'carry too far' abstraction is appropriately more argumentative in tone.

A number of instances are found in which, while the literal sense on which the primitive image was formed is again brought vividly into consciousness, a certain contrast is established between this individual newly-created sharpness and the dull and ordinary tone which the language unit carries in general currency. Lydgate speaks to Mr Bulstrode of 'the deep stamp which anxiety will make for a time even on the young and vigorous' (Ch. 67); Dorothea remembers how pretty is Lydgate's wife; 'every impression about Rosamond had cut deep' into her mind (Ch. 76). For the characters of the novel also these clichés have taken on a 'distinctness which is no longer reflection but feeling'. One may judge further that it is sometimes the novelist's intention so to re-word an image that it stands out with an awkward unexpectedness against the narrative background: 'It was an inference with a conspicuous handle to it, and had been easily drawn by indifferent observers, that Lydgate was in debt' (Ch. 58). As the original action involved in drawing an inference is firmly restored to the cliché-image, 'indifferent observers' are brought by casual curiosity into the movement of the story. That Lydgate has himself given a handle to his critics is suggested also through the visual image of the handle so conspicuous that it invites an experimental manipulation (Ch. 58). The author may re-word the cliché-image while at the same time extending and reinforcing it. Bulstrode, who 'had been used every day to taste the flavour of supremacy', is conscious 'that there was a deposit of uneasy presentiment in his wife's mind' (Ch. 68); his realization that she was passing beyond the stage of unsettled suspense may be combined here with the taste and flavour metaphor; there may also be in Bulstrode's mind some fear of finally drinking to the dregs the cup of humiliation. Of Dorothea we are told in the earlier part of the story (Ch. 10) that she cared nothing for learning as mere accomplishment. 'She did not want to deck herself with knowledge—to wear it loose from the nerves and blood that fed her action'—a sentence which has been revised in the manuscript, the first part written above an erasure, the second part inserted in the margin. We may judge the revision successful; form and content are finely interwoven. 'Deck herself' has a tone of literary pretentiousness which is properly set aside, while the striving for full expression within the second 'wearing' image is far removed from the crude derogation of the 'skin-deep' cliché which may seem to some readers to underlie it.

Countless small examples could be cited where the novelist is able to force the general language towards an individual effect precisely adapted to her narrative purpose. She comments on Lydgate's reading at the age of ten (Ch. 15), as 'neither milk for babes, nor any chalky mixture meant to pass for milk', using first, if I may so express it, the image-cliché in its current form (as applied to reading matter) to convey a superlative negation, and then at once watering down that superlative, by means of a newly-coined image, to a merely comparative sense; the books which the boy is reading are not even school-room adaptations pretending to be the strong-meat genuine thing. Because of the 'milk/strong-meat for babes' antithesis which is current in general language with pedagogic connotation, the 'chalk' of the new image (as well as glancing at the scandals of food adulterations) has in part the sense of blackboard chalk, and at the same time, in the Lydgate context, it is in addition the chalkiness of the medicine-bottle mixture; in this way the 'milk for babes' cliché becomes a visual (and bottled) image also, both colour and fluidity restored. When Fred Vincy takes to horse-trading, the author describes how the silence of Mr Horrock, 'the vet', helps 'to create the reputation of . . . an infinite fund of humour —too dry to flow and probably in a state of immovable crust' (Ch. 23). Here positive is made superlative; dryness and crustiness, carried to their logical conclusions, lose something of their general 'humour' connotation so as to enclose and support the infinite undiminished fund. Image may be made appropriate to image-maker as well as to the imaged object. There is a non-progressive prosiness in Mr Casaubon's hope that Carp will 'have to eat his own words with a good deal of indigestion', a figure supported by Casaubon's himself tasting the sweeter 'flavour of vengeance' and 'bitter savours of irritated jealousy' (Ch. 42). On the other hand, Ladislaw's swiftly thrown-off image, as he talks to Dorothea in Rome about the short-comings of Mr Casaubon's scholarship, his 'correcting mistakes' in work already so out-of-date that it will not bear examination, 'living', as Will expresses it, 'in a lumber-room and furbishing up broken-legged theories', has in its brisk alliteration a zest and enthusiasm however misplaced, which Casaubon has never known (Ch. 22). So too, within a confused mind an 'odd patchwork' of clichés may be combined into a single clouded image. We are told of Mrs Waule that notwithstanding her jealousy of the Vincys and of Mary Garth, 'there remained as the nethermost sediment in her mental shallows a persuasion that her brother Peter Featherstone could never leave his chief property away from his blood-relations: else, why had the Almighty carried off his two wives both childless, after he had gained so much by manganese and things?' (Ch. 12). 'Blood is thicker than water': at the bottom of her shallow mind lies the hope (built, unfortunately, not upon the rock but on sandy ground) that, in the last analysis, some trace of family solidity, some identity of plasma, will be found in the nethermost sediment of brother and sister. In contrast to this kind of damp, slow, sifting image there is an exhilarating speed in the description of how the 'gossip about Bulstrode spread through Middlemarch like the smell of fire' (Ch. 71); a complex of image-clichés is brought into play. The simple verb 'spread' in the 'fire' context may bring to mind the cliché-image 'like wildfire'; 'smell' suggests a shrewdness in discovering the long-suspected: in the generality of language we smell a rat, smell out a scandal; we know that there is 'no smoke without fire'. And in the individual language of the novel-world, since 'hardly anybody doubted that some scandalous reason or other was at the bottom of Bulstrode's liberality to Lydgate', we may even smell again through this pungent fire image those red herrings which Rosamond Vincy wished her brother not to have for his overlate breakfast (Ch. 11); we may remember also that her husband's 'professional and scientific ambition had no other relation' to her plans for social climbing 'than if they had been the fortunate discovery of an ill-smelling oil' (Ch. 58).

Language is enlivened and our pattern of expectancy broken by such devices as the occasional smooth 'hingeing together' of two quite ordinary images which, even though they contain an identical verbal element, belong in normal speech to wholly different situational contexts: in the Vincy's drawing-room, as Lydgate 'took his seat with easy confidence' on the other side of Rosamond, 'young Plymdale's jaw fell like a barometer towards the cheerless side of change' (Ch. 27). In this instance the word 'fell' is the hinge on which our attention pivots from the falling jaw (now a somewhat outdated image of chagrin and disappoint-ment) to the falling mercury. Once again the simile chosen does 'really illustrate the nature' of the thing compared. Young Plymdale's facial expression as accurately prognosticates his evening-long dejection as might the movement of a barometer; his falling jaw is to stay fallen for some considerable time. This by-play with the forms of language can be directed to more than mere amusement: in an apparently uncontroversial authorial statement the factor of surprise may be brilliantly exploited and the generality of social judgment firmly set aside. If we have been used to think of dough as an image of lumpish ignorance or failure—knowing perhaps the proverb which Shakespeare uses, 'My cake is dough', my project has failed—such a preconception is doubly challenged. Sir James, the author tells us, 'was made of excellent human dough', the superlative-pure (excellent) and the superlative-palliative (human) both preceding the figurative noun (Ch. 2); the jolt which ends the sentence lets us know that we are not henceforward to judge so harshly the potentialities of our fellows. Subtle variations of tone may be introduced within a short series of related images. Mrs Cadwallader (Ch. 6) speaks 'with the clearest chiselled utterance'; the countryside would have been 'somewhat duller if the Rector's lady had been less . . . of a skinflint'. Everywhere there is evidence of the tact and care with which the minor imagery is handled. When Dorothea (Ch. 4) hears from her sister of the servants' talk 'that Sir James was to marry the eldest Miss Brooke' she asks indignantly, ' "How can you let Tantripp talk such gossip to you, Celia?" . . . not the less angry because she had had a stifled presentment of the fact.' But in the final manuscript copy this last clause is struck out, evidently because the concrete action of the image must be in character, and the choking back of an awareness—suffocating even an abstraction—is a negation quite foreign to Dorothea's nature. Instead of this clause there is substituted the accepting image 'details asleep in her memory were now awakened to confirm the unwelcome revelation'.[11] Here there is no repudiation or inner conflict; sleeper and waker are part of the same thinking-feeling identity; the sleep is calm, the waking judgment clear. The interest of this manuscript corrrection prompts one to look again at Dorothea's cry at the climax of her story, 'What should I do—how should I act now, this very day, if I could clutch my own pain, and compel it to silence, and think of these three?' (Ch. 80). In this instance also we see that there is no stifling of the feelings; the 'I' is both actor and sufferer. The compressed image 'clutch my own pain . . .' seems to suggest at once the open wound and the child whose anguish is frightening to hear; the suffering child which is the pain is accepted as no less a factor in the personal identity than the strenuously active moral sense which is its adult counterpart.

ECONOMY OF THE IMAGE

Here as elsewhere the economy of the image intensifies the feeling, and it seems useful in this respect to compare George Eliot's practice as novelist with Herbert Spencer's notes on the theory of style and imagery (included in a review-article, 'The Philosophy of Style', published in the *Westminster Review*, of which George Eliot was then the editor, in the year 1852.[12] In this year she and Spencer were so much together that it was supposed they might be engaged).[13] Spencer has a good deal to say on the need for 'economizing the reader's or hearer's attention' and speaks of the importance of the 'choice and arrangement of the minor images out of which some larger thought is to be built'. He observes that the 'secret of producing a vivid impression' lies in selecting from a 'scene, or event described, those typical elements which carry many others along with them, and so, by saying a few things but suggesting many, to abridge the description'. Undoubtedly George Eliot has this secret. In *Middlemarch* especially the superiority of specific over general terms is constantly brought before us; a large segment of experience is represented through the single salient detail. Such a method can be very effective when the author has general comments to make: wit is a great abridgement. We are told, for example, of how within the old provincial society as the boundaries of social intercourse shifted, 'people denied aspirates, gained wealth, and fastidious gentlemen stood for boroughs' (Ch. 11). One detail of visual imagery may suffice for many: 'Lydgate's hair never became white. He died when he was only fifty, leaving his wife and children provided for by a heavy insurance on his life. He had gained an excellent practice . . .' etc. The one negative statement stands for all that follows: Lydgate does not live to be old, but he offers no appearance of being prematurely aged by sorrow at what he regards as his failure; others see him as successful in the world; his looks do not call forth that veneration which would be due to one who had given a long life to arduous medical research. Varying subjective experience of known and measurable reality can be vividly expressed in concrete terms. As the novelist compares her range with that of an earlier master, the extensiveness of earlier time is measured against an ever-increasing scale: 'Fielding lived when the days were longer . . . when summer afternoons were spacious, and the clock ticked slowly in the winter evenings (Ch. 15). For Ladislaw, on the other hand, as a child enduring poverty, the day itself is the natural unit; 'my father had made himself known to Mr Casaubon', he tells Dorothea, 'and that was my last hungry day' (Ch. 37).

What a character thinks and feels about a number of complex factors within a longish narrative sequence can be very economically shown through the image which he forms of one particular moment in that sequence. Mr Brooke, in his talk to Dorothea of poaching and game-preserving, tells of how the Methodist preacher, brought up before the bench 'for knocking down a hare that came across his path' and written off as a hypocrite by one of the magistrates, pleaded comically enough 'that he thought the Lord had sent him and his wife a good dinner'. Brooke's unspoken acceptance of the sincerity of that plea is summed up in his comment, 'But really, when I came to think of it, I couldn't help liking that the fellow should have a bit of hare to say grace over' (Ch. 39). Far from supposing, for instance, that the preacher and his wife find poached hare especially tasty, Brooke's fancy stays itself at the moment of private and domestic religious ceremony with which their illegitimate meal begins.

The single adjective 'broad' in the closing phrase of a chapter, 'and they went along the broad corridor together' (Ch. 42) sums up in a final visual image Dorothea's resolution of a long and changing struggle. In this chapter Casaubon has 'for the first time found himself looking into the eyes of death' and shrinking from Dorothea's pity has 'allowed her pliant arm to cling with difficulty against his rigid arm'. In 'rebellious anger' Dorothea asks herself 'What is the use of anything I do? . . .'

Like one who has lost his way and is weary, she sat and saw as in one glance all the paths of her young hope which she should never find again . . . she saw her own and her husband's solitude—how they walked apart so that she was obliged to survey him. If he had drawn her towards him, she would never have surveyed him—never have said, 'Is he worth living for?' but would have felt him simply a part of her own life.

Gradually the energy of her anger inspires 'a resolved submission'; 'when the house was still . . . she opened her door gently and stood outside in the darkness' waiting for Mr Casaubon. As he spoke to her 'with a gentle surprise', with a 'kind quiet melancholy', she 'put her hand into her husband's, and they went along the broad corridor together'. Lowick Manor is spacious and the corridor is broad in actuality: Rosamond Vincy has teased Lydgate about his medical visits to the house . . . 'at least you go through wide corridors and have the scent of rose-leaves everywhere' (Ch. 31). But clearly also, in relation to Dorothea's earlier images of the lost way, 'all the paths of her young hope' and 'how they walked apart', the 'broad corridor' is part of her subjective awareness; its width is taken note of because she and her husband are moving along it together; in their shared gentleness marriage seems purposeful and less constricting.

One last point here. 'To have a specific style', says Spencer, 'is to be poor in speech.'[14] Even though the novelist seems generally to select her images in the belief (to use her own words) that 'emotion links itself with particulars, and only in a faint and secondary manner with abstractions',[15] the reader has no feeling that her talent is confined to any single method of working. There is no 'repeated production of the same effects';[16] abstractions are sometimes very simply and strikingly employed. We are told in the Prelude of how Theresa walked out from Avila one morning hand-in-hand with her still smaller brother 'until domestic reality met them in the shape of uncles, and turned them back from their great resolve'. It is difficult to comment briefly enough on the economy of this statement. The words sound friendly as the uncles, no doubt, looked friendly, but just as adults, even though recognizably uncles, can stop a child's way forward, not by talk or argument, but simply by being too big, so also (to women who are often childlike, often treated like children) 'reality' can be even more of a blockage for taking a friendly shape; the accompanying adjective 'domestic' only seems to make the reality smaller but does not really make it so. A simpler example is found when Fred Vincy agrees with Mary Garth that he is 'idle and extravagant' and tries to get from her some admission of her affection for him while she remains 'provokingly mistress of the situation'. She 'looked up with some roguishness at Fred, and that look of hers was very dear to him, though the eyes were nothing more than clear windows where observation sat laughingly' (Ch. 14). The somewhat unusual personification of this last phrase (a manuscript addition) is perfectly in context. When Dorothea comes to the summer-house to give her answer and later in the day, in her delirium, asks Lydgate to explain everything to her husband and tell him that she is ready to promise, the chapter ends, magnificently, with the sentence 'But the silence in her husband's ear was never more to be broken' (Ch. 48). Emotion and particulars are wiped out; one quality stands for a whole situation.

STRATEGIES OF INDIRECTION

Of her delight in the play of language George Eliot tells us little but she speaks often and with a certain Puritan energy of the novelist's moral purpose. From these moral pronouncements we can perhaps learn something of her theory of imagery and language. It seems that art is for her a clearer image of life; in her own words, it is 'a mode of amplifying experience and extending our contact with our fellowmen';[17] the range of vision is wider and the focus sharper; through the 'higher sensibility' of the writer our understanding and sympathy are increased.[18] She believes with Lewes that the 'true purpose of Knowledge is the regulation of our Conduct'[19] and that effective knowledge, whether gained from life or art, comes best through feeling. In 'Leaves from a Notebook' (published in 1884), when considering 'modes of telling a story' and 'the superior mastery of images and pictures in grasping the attention', she notes 'the fact that our earliest, strongest impressions, our most intimate convictions, are simply images added to more or less of sensation. These are the primitive instruments of thought.'[20] Lewes holds to the doctrine that 'all cognition is primarily emotion'[21] and she expresses a similar idea in one of her letters—'to receive deep impressions is the foundation of all true mental power'.[22] It seems, if we expand this characteristic double-cliché figure, that the strenuous, masculine, shovel-by-shovel effort towards intellectual foundation-laying works through and is complemented by the natural 'give' of human clay. Progress rests upon a willing submission to innate susceptibility of feeling. One thinks of the contrast between Dorothea at the beginning of the story, 'taking her usual place in the pretty sitting-room . . . bent on finishing a plan for some buildings (a kind of work she delighted in)' and of George Eliot when *Middlemarch* is finished, and she is 'thoroughly at peace about it', not because she is convinced that it is perfect but because she has given it what she could. 'When a subject has begun to grow in me', she writes to Alexander Main, 'I suffer terribly until it has wrought itself out— become a complete organism', and, later in the same letter, 'Nothing mars the receptivity more than eager construction, as I know to my own cost':[23] submission to the nature of the material, in life as well as in novel-writing, is evidently reckoned of greater value than over-confident efforts at quickly won control. It is scarcely necessary to emphasize the importance of imagery for the writer who believes in this way that intellectual growth rests largely on the acquiring of intuitive knowledge and who counts herself most fully successful when 'the emotion which stirred [her] in writing is repeated in the mind of the reader'.[24]

I have suggested earlier that examination of her minor imagery enables us to see quite quickly with what subtle control she plays upon the figurative language of ordinary life so as to bring about a writer-reader communication somewhat below the level of our immediate consciousness. It is however equally clear that as regards the larger issues of this kind of moral therapy there can be few short cuts. What life or the novel teaches, the reader learns quite slowly; those truths which the novelist would wish to have most deeply felt may be better expressed in other ways than the direct verbal statement. We can be certain that she will choose those ways with care. It is even possible that the clearer image of life which she offers to the readers of *Middlemarch* is significantly different from real life as she knows it. In thus considering some few instances of her strategies of indirection it is of some interest to observe that whereas George Eliot herself can write in one of her letters of words being 'helpless borrowings and echoes, giving no description of what has gone on within the speaker',[25] the reader of *Middlemarch* is not in general required to take note of the difficulty of verbalizing complex experience. Most of the characters for much of the time show a remarkable command of words and tone; the intractability of language as a medium is considerably played down. A detailed consideration of the reasons for this would be out of place here but it seems to me to be part of George Eliot's larger image strategy not to allow us any opportunity to share in the difficulties of the novel writer. She seems consciously to have intended that whatever sense of effort is produced in the reader, whatever awareness of strain and suffering, is to come exclusively from our identification with the different characters of the story.

'Cognition is primarily emotion'; the writer's own generalizing didactic statements are not made too early and they are very carefully placed. We find, for example, that the author's realistic appraisal of that infantile egocentricity which is our common starting-point does not come until about a quarter of the way through the novel, on the day when Dorothea, in Rome

had begun to see that she had been under a wild illusion in expecting a response to her feeling from Mr Casaubon, and she had felt the waking of a presentiment that there might be a sad consciousness in his life which made as great a need on his side as on her own.

We are all of us born in moral stupidity, taking the world as an udder to feed our supreme selves: Dorothea had early begun to emerge from that stupidity, but yet it had been easier to her to imagine how she would devote herself to Mr Casaubon, and become wise and strong in his strength and wisdom, than to conceive with that distinctness which is no longer reflection but feeling—an idea wrought back to the directness of sense, like the solidity of objects—that he had an equivalent centre of self, whence the lights and shadows must always fall with a certain difference. (Ch. 21)

What may well represent George Eliot's ideal in her use of imagery, to have us 'conceive with that distinctness which is no longer reflection but feeling', is here presented in an image of Dorothea's spiritual growth, a growth even now scarcely begun—the 'had' in 'yet it had been easier' seems not merely to refer to the past but to carry some tinge also of the Casaubon-style subjunctive, a distancing of future possibility. We may notice further that this impressive chapter-ending, epoch-ending sentence has been so constructed that its most important phrase, 'to conceive with that distinctness which is no longer reflection but feeling', is merely the dismissed comparison (than which daydreaming of sacrifice and of wisdom is far easier). It is not given prominence of place as subject or object of the sentence; it is not set out as a conscious aim either for Dorothea or for ourselves; the blind infant mammal cannot know the maturity towards which it moves; none of us can *think* what it is like to feel-rather-than-think in sympathy with others. And if, in some sense, the imagery of the novel is to be our training-ground, even through the placing of this didactic 'We are all' statement, a certain exercise is offered. Having watched 'poor Dorothea' acting under the wild illusion that has carried her off to Rome with one 'no better than a mummy', are we not more adept than she in our thinking-feeling relations? George Eliot's sentence order makes this doubtful: Dorothea has begun to see beyond her own needs before we are brought back to humanity's primitive condition of unlimited oral demand!

It is obvious also that long before Dorothea has begun to feel that Mr Casaubon has 'an equivalent centre of self' and long before 'we are all of us' confronted with and left to think about this summarising paragraph, we have been under subtle linguistic pressure to feel-rather-than-think from many such equivalent centres. So too before we have been required to encounter any derogatory first-person plural generalizations there has been practice with a number of second-person singular hypotheses; after the interest of taking on a number of different personalities within the action of the story, the reader is ready for a certain attempt to carry over experience gained. The remarkable ease and swiftness with which George Eliot conditions us in *Middlemarch* to this habit of splitting allegiance and changing identity may be noticed especially in the opening pages of the novel: we are led, first of all, through her use of the 'you' pronoun, to adopt the attitude of the ideal reader and then, while this ideal reader follows the narrative, we take on, in addition, from time to time, the changing image of one who is living the action. The first 'you' (of sentence 5) represents a blending of the indefinite pronoun, the reader who is being given information, and the reader who, along with the author, is taking trouble to find information, to seek out reasons, in a leisurely way, for what has already, in the first twenty or so lines of the chapter, been observed, compared and differentiated—'the plain dressing' of Miss Brooke and her sister Celia: 'the Brooke connections, though not exactly aristocratic, were unquestionably "good": if you inquired backward for a generation or two, you would not find any yard-measuring or parcel-tying forefathers.'

The fourth paragraph of the chapter opens with the ringing rhetorical question 'And how should Dorothea not marry?' which at once splits the readers' allegiance, giving us two opposing sides to support in any argument that is to follow. The second 'you', nameless, male, 'wary' (essentially yard-measuring), represents one faction only in suggesting an answer to this question. He 'naturally' thinks twice before making Dorothea an offer. 'Such a wife might awaken you some fine morning with a new scheme for the application of her income. . . .' This 'you' has clearly in mind the potentially divergent interests of 'you' and 'her' and it is perhaps worth noting also with what skilful lack of emphasis the author suggests to us that this imagined marriage is considered only in its financial aspect; no sexual union forms part of the hypothetical relationship: the last clause before this 'might awaken you' sentence has the young lady 'sitting up at night to read old theological books!'

When the third 'you' comes, one page later, Dorothea, surprisingly enough, is also calculating, but rather tentatively, and not the risks, of course, but the profit of matrimony. That Sir James Chettam

should be regarded as a suitor to herself would have seemed to her a ridiculous irrelevance . . . an amiable handsome baronet, who said, 'Exactly' to her remarks even when she expressed uncertainty,—how could he affect her as a lover? The really delightful marriage must be that where your husband was a sort of father, and could teach you even Hebrew, if you wished it.

While the 'you' and 'your' of this last sentence take the participating reader into the heart of Dorothea's unspoken 'childlike ideas', the split-off observing reader is bound to carry forward the author's question 'how could he affect her as a lover?' from the actual disregarded suitor to the imagined 'sort of father' husband. And this feminine 'you', it may be noted, does not accord to its partner separate pronoun status, does not imagine the possibility that his wishes might run counter to her own.

Little more than a page further on, as Celia is tentatively proposing the division of the jewels, her face 'had the shadow of a pouting expression in it, the full presence of the pout being kept back by an habitual awe of Dorothea and principle; two associated facts which might show a mysterious electricity if you touched them incautiously'.This single use of the 'you' pronoun involves the reader not so much in movement as in holding back from movement; watching Celia's facial expression we sense to the full the caution which controls it; our training in the kinaesthetic image has begun.

LIFE-LANGUAGE AND NOVEL-LANGUAGE

George Eliot is well aware that no direct exhibition of moral bias can make a book really moral in its influence. In her article on Goethe's *Wilhelm Meister* (1855) she describes how the child listening to a story will lose interest as soon as the teller betrays 'symptoms of an intention to moralize, or to turn the current of facts towards a personal application'. 'One grand reason of this is, that the child is aware you are talking *for it* instead of *from yourself*, so that instead of carrying it along in a stream of sympathy with your own interest in the story, you give it the impression of contriving coldly, and talking artificially'.[26] Some part of the reader's conviction that the writer of *Middlemarch* is talking from herself comes, no doubt, from the obvious autobiographical elements in the story. Dorothea's unfulfilled aspiration 'to make her life greatly effective' and her being 'only known in a certain circle as a wife and mother' (Finale) could serve as an image of the lives of many Victorian women who knew in their own youth, as did the novelist herself, the 'active conscience' and 'great mental need' (Ch. 3).

The young Mary Anne Evans, of course, had a much more

active brain and greater mental powers than the young Dorothea. Even while 'shut up in a farmhouse in the remote country' (to quote from her *Life* by J. W. Cross) 'she was always prosecuting an active intellectual life of her own'.[27] But Cross speaks also of how once when he was urging her to write her autobiography, she said, half sighing, half smiling, 'The only thing I should care much to dwell on would be the absolute despair I suffered from of ever being able to achieve anything. No one could ever have felt greater despair, and a knowledge of this might be a help to some other struggler.'[28]

Other correspondences between the emotional lives of Dorothea and George Eliot are more fully apparent to later readers. Dorothea, about to marry Ladislaw, has 'prefigured to herself, even with exaggeration, the disgust of her friends' (Ch. 84); in Celia's words, 'nobody can think where you will live: where can you go?' Celia 'cannot think how it all came about' and Dorothea cannot tell her . . . 'you would have to feel with me, else you would never know'. Sir James consents to a reconciliation after the birth of Dorothea's first child. George Eliot's brother, Isaac Evans, wrote to her again after an interval of twenty-four years when, after the death of Lewes, she was legally married to Mr Cross.[29]

One has seldom the impression in *Middlemarch* that the writer is talking artificially or self-consciously; when she says 'we are all' she means it deeply. The vocabulary of the novel has worn well; very few of her words strike us at the present time as being odd or old-fashioned. When, for example, Dorothea cannot 'reconcile the anxieties of a spiritual life involving eternal consequences, with a keen interest in guimp and artificial protrusions of drapery' (Ch. 1), it is clear that the word 'guimp' has been deliberately chosen as a type of the non-persistent. The only remarkable thing about the grammar of the novel is the fineness of its use. So, for instance, the indefinite adjective 'some' adds a touch of muted irony to the description of how Lydgate feels that there 'was another attraction in his profession: it wanted reform, and gave a man an opportunity for some indignant resolve' (Ch. 15). The reader is prompted perhaps to compare Lydgate's and Dorothea's conditions: Lydgate needs and has

found a channel into which a certain apportionment of his somewhat superior intellectual and emotional energy may be run off.
The author's sure and economical use of Midland dialect adds
to her imagery within the novel a certain flavour of conservative
provincialism. Through the use of such homely, localized language, a whole series of type-situations can be suggested in
short phrase or single word. When Mary Garth is overjoyed to
hear from her father that Fred is to manage Stone Court, '"Ah,
but mind you" said Caleb, turning his head warningly, "I must
take it on *my* shoulders, and be responsible, and see after everything . . . Fred had need be careful."' (Ch. 86). This fixed-form
phrase '. . . but mind you' is still in use in exactly Caleb's sense,
when an older speaker warns a younger that opposite considera-
tions have positively to be taken into account. If one may suppose
that the novelist intends the title *Middlemarch* to present, as one
facet of its meaning, a Pilgrim's Progress imperative, Caleb's
phrase, I think, could stand as the regularly used, unbookish
variant of this summing-up image. Lydgate's vision of research
'provisionally framing its object and correcting it to more and
more exactness of relation' (Ch. 16), as also Dorothea's promise
to learn 'what everything costs' (Ch. 83), although very different
in tone, come within the same semantic range. In Midland speech
'us', used for 'me', after an imperative verb, constitutes a strong
reminder of a claim to equal treatment, so that when Raffles
greets Bulstrode with the words 'Come, shake us by the hand'
(Ch. 53), this 'us' usage images in little all the repeated demands
that Bulstrode may anticipate. Brother Solomon and Mrs Waule,
while Featherstone lies dying, sit every day for hours in the
large wainscotted parlour 'without other calculable occupation
than that of observing the cunning Mary Garth (who was so
deep that she could be found out in nothing)' (Ch. 32). In
familiar spoken language this adjective 'deep' implies envious
respect as well as a suspicious hostility towards someone who
might be reckoned, on outward appearance, not much to be
taken note of. As used here the 'deep' image (which has been
added to the final draft of the manuscript) may well carry a
reminder of the obverse situation when Lydgate, who on his
visit to Featherstone 'hardly noticed' Miss Garth, hears from

Farebrother, without 'caring to know more' how 'she gauges everybody' (Ch. 17). Perhaps too from the literal sense of deep in relation to the 'brown patch' Mary, a further questioning reference ripples back to the Prelude's image of the 'ducklings in the brown pond'. Mary and Fred stay on among their Middlemarch neighbours to achieve 'a solid mutual happiness'; the pond which is shallow at its edges may have sufficient depth and freshness at its centre.

It happens very occasionally in reading *Middlemarch* that one's attention is caught by an image which, used by a novelist of the present time, would appear distasteful, contrived or literary, and it is accordingly of some interest to confirm that these images also are part of George Eliot's ordinary letter-writing language. Evidently their currency has been somewhat devalued by the passage of time. Whereas 'Lydgate's spots of common-ness lay in the complexion of his prejudices' (Ch. 15), no hero of our time, as far as I know, has merely figurative pimples, yet George Eliot can describe herself as figuratively sallow. While her 'warm, enthusiastic husband . . . is a miracle of freedom from all author's jealousy and all suspicion', she confesses to a fear 'that the Casaubon-tints are not quite foreign' to her own 'mental complexion'.[30] The non-literal verb 'tax' at the present day seems to have lost all connection with property or capital, so that when the novelist writes of one's self-satisfaction as 'an untaxed kind of property which it is very unpleasant to find depreciated' (Ch. 16), the metaphor appears awkward and unclear. A similar usage is found in a letter written after a 'gastric irritation' (6 October, 1871): 'I think my complaint had nothing to do with brain-work, except so far as this has been diffused over my life at the expense of my bodily capital; for I have not been taxing myself—indeed for many months I have been too ailing to do more than an apology for a morning's work.' The first chapter of *Middlemarch* ends with Celia pardoning her sister:

Since they could remember, there had been a mixture of criticism and awe in the attitude of Celia's mind towards her elder sister. The younger had always worn a yoke; but is there any yoked creature without its private opinions?

The 'yoke' as an image is too ponderous for the spoken language of today; for George Eliot it suggests an interwoven ambivalence of mutual dependency, as in this same letter (6 October 1871) which tells of their old servants' leaving after ten years' service:

We should never have dismissed them, and we looked forward to taking care of them when they were too old to work. But their oddities were a yoke which we were certain would get heavier with the years, and since they could think of going we are contented now that they should go. [31]

These few instances excepted, it does not seem in *Middlemarch* that George Eliot is in any way 'contriving coldly' in her handling of the minor metaphorical language which she has so much at her disposal. One has rather the sense that the full energy of the writer's thinking and feeling life is flowing into her novel-language; a tentative comparison of a little of the *Middlemarch* imagery with the image-language of her letters and her reading confirms this impression. If in the novel the use of any particular image were thought of as somewhat overdone, it would, I suppose, be that of sunshine and sunlight as representing hopefulness and warmth of purpose: even when Mr Casaubon on his visit to Tipton Grange seemed 'more and more bent' on making Dorothea talk to him, 'on drawing her out', his face in looking at her 'was often lit up by a smile like pale wintry sunshine' (Ch. 3). It is interesting to see however that in the novelist's own life sunshine is equally symbolic—dramatically evocative of a sense of well-being. 'I cannot feel hopeful without the sunlight' she says in one of her letters,[32] and elsewhere she speaks of 'the sunshine being to me the greatest visible good of life—what I call the wealth of life, after love and trust'.[33] Perhaps it is not surprising that the word 'ardent' is found so frequently in *Middlemarch* as a term of praise; one remembers too that the writer was sent away to school at the age of five and that over half a century later 'what chiefly remained in her recollection about this very early school-life was the difficulty of getting near enough the fire in winter, to become thoroughly warmed, owing to the circle of girls forming round too narrow a fireplace. This suffering from cold was the beginning of a low general state of health.'[34] Again, when Dorothea is to leave Middlemarch and go to live in London, the hard reality of her renunciation is measured in the despairing directness of Celia's question 'How can you always live in a street?' (Ch. 84). George Eliot herself felt in the full Wordsworthian sense 'the blessedness of being in the country'.[35] Writing from Shottermill, for instance (14 August 1871), she describes her evening walks with Lewes, 'About six or half-past we walk on to the commons and see the great sky over our head.'[36] After the death of Lewes's twenty-five year old son, Thornton (19 October 1869), when she was so much 'shattered in mind and body . . .',[37] 'nothing but the deep calm of fields and woods'[38] could have restored her. So, in the novel, Mr Cadwallader, although 'very plain and rough in his exterior', has 'that solid imperturbable ease and good-humour which . . . like great grassy hills in the sunshine, quiets even an irritated egoism, and makes it rather ashamed of itself' (Ch. 8).

Other correspondences may perhaps be noted between life-language and novel-language. A few weeks before Thornton's death, George Eliot writes: 'He is going on well, we think, in his slow way. . . . His face has more than ever of the wizened look that has come instead of its old beauty, and that pains me to see; I cannot shake off the impression it creates in me of slow withering.'[39] In *Middlemarch* we find the youthful withering and the pain of the onlooker when, after the reading of Mr Featherstone's will, Mary Garth 'met Fred in the hall, and now for the first time had the courage to look at him. He had that withered sort of paleness which will sometimes come on young faces' (Ch. 35).

Much of the emotional suffering which we feel in *Middlemarch* comes to us through the physical image; we are made aware of pain not as a simple collective term but in its different qualities and gradations; it has its own progressive modes. Physical pain arising from mental stress was part of George Eliot's working life; Lydgate's 'creeping self-despair', his sense that there was lying around him 'a grand existence in thought and effective action' which yet he could not reach (Ch. 64), seems to have been known also to the creating novelist. George Eliot describes Lydgate, after the failure of his application to Bulstrode and the execution for debt in his house, as feeling 'bruised and shattered, and there was a dark line under his eyes which Rosamond had not seen before' (Ch. 69). Lewes (in a letter to Blackwood, 13 February 1872) describes George Eliot's despair and 'self tormenting': 'Reading "Felix Holt" the other morning made her *thin* with misery, so deeply impressed was she with the fact that she could never write like that again and that what is now in hand is rinsings of the cask.'[40]

Lewes himself shows a fine command of the analogical image. In reading his work one feels that George Eliot's novels are what they are partly through her good fortune in having so gifted a prose writer as the life-companion of her best working years. When Dorothea 'is discovered in a fit of weeping six weeks after her wedding' the novelist generalizes her experience with the image 'whatever else remained the same, the light had changed, and you cannot find the pearly dawn at noonday' (Ch. 20). In his *Physiology of Common Life* Lewes uses a similar image in an opposite sense when considering man's general consciousness: 'We do not see the stars at noonday, yet they shine. . . . There is a general illumination from the sun and stars, but of this we are seldom aware, because our attention falls upon the illumined objects, brighter or darker than this general tone.'[41] The following is a typical passage from his chapter on 'Sleep and Dreams'.

Look at that child: wearied with play, he has thrown himself upon the ground, and, resting a flushed cheek upon one arm, he lies there breathing equably, with motionless limbs, eyes closed, brain shut out from the lights and noises around him. If you touch his hand, he will withdraw it; if you tickle his cheek, he will impatiently turn his head aside; but even should he turn his whole body round, he will not, perhaps, open his eyes—will not *know* who it is, or what it is, that molests him; he will not awake. His mind, engaged in dreams, is disengaged from external things: they may make impressions on him, excite sensations in him, but these sensations are not wrought up into knowledge.[42]

Image and argument are made concrete and, through the

characteristic 'if you' phrase, energy of reader and writer is concentrated on ordered enquiry and observation. The condition of our waking life is to have sensations 'wrought up into knowledge', and, as with George Eliot and other thinkers of their day who had set aside the old forms of Christian belief, the verb 'wrought' (an archaic past tense of the infinitive 'work') seems to have taken on some sense of the god-like energy of man's mental powers, as if in his ability to correlate there lies his true divinity. It carries with it that force on which, for example, Lewes comments when he writes of Goethe's *Prometheus* fragment 'Godlike energy is seen only in creation; what we can *do* we *are*; our strength is measured by our plastic power.'[43]

SPINOZA's 'ETHICS'

Lewes and Goethe before him came upon Spinoza's *Ethics* with something of the same effect that Lydgate as a boy opened the volume of an old encyclopaedia at the anatomy section: 'the moment of vocation had come . . . the world was made new to him. . . . From that hour Lydgate felt the growth of an intellectual passion' (Ch. 15). In his *Life and Works of Goethe* which he was writing in Weimar in 1854, at the time when George Eliot was translating Spinoza's *Ethics*, Lewes quotes Goethe's words: 'Of what I read *in* the work, and of what I read *into* it, I can give no account, but I found in it a sedative for my passions and it seemed to unveil a clear, broad view over the material and moral world.'[44]

Lewes says of himself: 'It was the casual citation of a passage from Spinoza which made my youth restless, and to this day I remember the aspect of the page where it appeared, and the revolution in thought which it effected.'

George Eliot's translation of Spinoza's *Ethics* is as yet unpublished but she has an interesting comment in one of her letters on Bray's project (1849) for printing an earlier translation of this work (which had been offered by an American):

If you are anxious to publish the translation in question I could, after a few months, finish the Tractatus Theologico-Politicus to keep it

company—but I confess to you, that I think you would do better to
abstain from printing a translation. What is wanted in English is not a
translation of Spinoza's works, but a true estimate of his life and system.
After one has rendered his Latin faithfully into English, one feels that
there is another yet more difficult process of translation for the reader
to effect, and that the only mode of making Spinoza accessible to a
larger number is to study his books, then shut them and give an analysis. [45]

One mode she was later to find seems to have been the writing
of *Middlemarch*; even the student who has 'not read much' of
Spinoza and the metaphysicians is bound to be impressed by the
'process of translation' she is able to effect. Spinoza's ideas have
been judged far too modern to have any effect on his seventeenth-
century contemporaries. He states, for example, that 'experience,
no less than reason, teaches that men believe themselves free
solely because they are conscious of their actions and ignorant of
the causes by which they are determined'. [46] It is self-knowledge,
to be gained through the exercise of the human intellect, which
will give them liberty; release from the bondage of the irrational
sets men's energies free. Fragmentary quotation will not serve,
of course, to bring out the main force of Spinoza's rigorously
ordered propositions (as, for instance, 'The more perfect a
thing is . . . the more it acts and the less it suffers'[47]) and I quote
therefore from an article by J. A. Froude in the *Westminster
Review* (1855), of which George Eliot said 'I don't at all agree
with Froude's own views, but I think his account of Spinoza's
doctrines admirable.'[48] Froude expands Spinoza's sentences on
adequate and inadequate ideas as affecting the human mind:

While we are governed by outward temptations, by the casual pleasures, the fortunes or the misfortunes of life, we are but instruments,
yielding ourselves to be acted upon as the animal is acted on by its
appetites, or the inanimate matter by the laws which bind it—we are
slaves. . . . So far, on the contrary, as we know clearly what we do, as
we understand what we are, and direct our conduct not by the passing
emotion of the moment, but by a grave, clear, and constant knowledge
of what is really good, so far we are said to act—we are ourselves the
spring of our own activity—we desire the genuine well-being of our
entire nature. [49]

Such a doctrine is clearly of central relevance to the 'allegory' of *Middlemarch*: Dorothea's progress in self-knowledge is an image of that progress to which the novelist would have us all attain; the accompanying minor imagery shows us the struggle (in Spinoza's words) to 'form a clear and distinct idea'[50] of confused and strong emotion, and the struggle ends with the habit of active thought established. We are told of Dorothea, as she sits crying in Rome: 'the mental act that was struggling forth into clearness was a self-accusing cry' (Ch. 20). At Lowick, as she talks to Will, she is strangely quiet: 'She was no longer struggling against the perception of facts, but adjusting herself to their clearest perception'; she now looks 'steadily at her husband's failure' (Ch. 37). At the climax of her story 'active thought' and 'vivid sympathetic experience returned to her now as a power: it asserted itself as acquired knowledge asserts itself and will not let us see as we saw in the day of our ignorance'. She asks Tantripp 'for her lighter mourning' from the wish to acknowledge 'that she had not the less an active life before her because she had buried a private joy' (Ch. 80). Casaubon, by contrast, finds it 'necessary to use the utmost caution' about his eyesight; he believes that 'We must not inquire too curiously into motives. . . . We must keep the germinating grain away from the light' (Ch. 2). The 'muffled suggestions of consciousness' that his way was lost among 'the rows of notebooks' it has hitherto been possible for him to explain away as 'mere fancy' (Ch. 20). Ladislaw judges harshly of the wrong which Casaubon had done to Dorothea in marrying her: 'A man was bound to know himself better than that.' When Dorothea speaks to him of Ladislaw's claim upon him, it is 'in the darkness' that Casaubon requests her never again to assume 'a judgement on subjects beyond' her scope (Ch. 37). Many such instances can be cited. Hearing that Lydgate 'had become the centre of infamous suspicions . . . it would have required a great deal of disentangling reflection, such as had never entered into Rosamond's life, for her in these moments to feel that her trouble was less than if her husband had been certainly known to have done something criminal' (Ch. 75). There is the comment in a later chapter 'We are on a perilous margin when we begin to look passively at our future selves. . . . Poor Lydgate was inwardly groaning on that margin, and Will was arriving at it' (Ch. 79).

I have spoken earlier of the subtle linguistic pressure by which the writer compels the reader, as in the first chapter of the novel, to feel-rather-than-think from a number of different centres of self. We are shown also throughout the story how the various characters form, as it were, different images of reality, giving attention—perhaps exclusive attention—to those narrowly limited elements of the general situation which belong to their particular preoccupations. Very many such instances are found, some brief and readily quotable, some set out at greater length with more complexity of character involvement. Celia 'is fonder of geraniums' (Ch. 10); Mary Garth's 'sewing is exquisite; it is the nicest thing' that Rosamond Vincy knows about her (Ch. 36). Mrs Garth's eldest son Christy 'who held it the most desirable thing in the world to be a tutor, to study all literatures . . . and who was an incorporate criticism' on poor Fred Vincy, 'a sort of object-lesson given him by the educational mother', stood himself 'not much higher than Fred's shoulder'. This made it the harder that he should be held superior for he 'was always as simple as possible, and thought no more of Fred's disinclination to scholarship than of a giraffe's' (Ch. 52).

It can be a measure of the change in personal circumstances that a character's view of reality changes; 'Celia's marriage seemed more serious than it used to do' (Ch. 28). The feelings of the moment may determine which one of many unimportant factors is taken note of; in electing to describe one detail rather than another the novelist enters into the changing mood of a character. When Sir James, early in the story, jumps off his horse to offer Dorothea the tiny Maltese puppy, he is described as 'raising his hat and showing his sleekly-waving blond hair'. The tone of the passage suggests that 'sleekly-waving' is held against him because 'Miss Brooke was annoyed at the interruption' (Ch. 3). The notable economy of imagery thus effected (as in the 'broad corridor' example mentioned earlier) rests on the assumption that the facts of consciousness are relative rather than absolute; in Lewes's paraphrase 'an idea is a state of the ideator'.[51] Spinoza states that by the term 'idea' he understands a 'conception' and that he used 'conception rather than perception because the word perception seems to indicate that the mind is passive in relation to the object'. The word 'conception' on the other hand 'seems to indicate the action of the mind'.[52] Lewes speaks of the great importance to contemporary psychology of this idea that 'the mind does not contemplate forms as the eye sees them—that the mind is not *apart* from its perceptions, but that it *is the perceptions*—that a perception is a *state of the percipient*, and that mind is the collective unity of these various states'.[53]

'This immortal discovery belongs', he thinks, 'to Hume; though Spinoza had, in his way, also foreseen it.' Elsewhere Lewes speaks of Spinoza 'anticipating modern psychology' in his statement 'that each person judges of things according to the disposition of his brain, or rather accepts the affections of his imagination as real things'.[54] So, for instance, in *Middlemarch* George Eliot tells us

We are all of us imaginative in some form or other, for images are the brood of desire; and poor old Featherstone, who laughed much at the way in which others cajoled themselves, did not escape the fellowship of illusion. (Ch. 34)

The 'mirror' images of the philosophers have a central place in the *Middlemarch* imagery of human egoism; the 'equivalent centre of self, whence the lights and shadows must always fall with a certain difference' (Ch. 21) derives, it has been pointed out, from a 'pregnant little fact' shown to the novelist by an 'eminent philosopher' among her friends.

Your pier-glass or extensive surface of polished steel made to be rubbed by a housemaid, will be minutely and multitudinously scratched in all directions; but place now against it a lighted candle as a centre of illumination, and lo! the scratches will seem to arrange themselves in a fine series of concentric circles round that little sun. It is demonstrable that the scratches are going everywhere impartially, and it is only your candle which produces the flattering illusion of a concentric arrangement, its light falling with an exclusive optical selection. These things are a parable. The scratches are events, and the candle is the egoism of any person now absent—of Miss Vincy, for example. (Ch. 27)

The 'eminent philosopher' of this paragraph may well be Lewes himself. He quotes a very striking 'mirror' image from Francis Bacon's *Novum Organum* when arguing against what he regards as Spinoza's fundamental error. Spinoza, says Lewes.

lays it down as a fundamental rule, that the correct definition of a thing expresses the nature of that thing, and nothing but its nature. We cannot but admire the consistency of this: he grapples boldly with the very difficulty of the science he is endeavouring to establish. It is obvious that, to know things which are *beyond* appearances, . . . which transcend the sphere of sense—we must know them as they *are*, . . . and not as they are *under the conditions of sense*. Spinoza at once pronounces that we can so know them. He says: whatever I clearly know is true; true not merely in reference to my conception of it, but in reference to the thing known. In other words, the mind is a mirror reflecting things as they are. . . . Now this doctrine, forced upon Des Cartes and Spinoza, and implied in the very nature of their inquiries . . . mistakes a relative truth for an universal one. There can be no doubt that—*as regards myself*—consciousness is the clear and articulate voice of truth; but it by no means follows, therefore, that—*as regards not-self*—consciousness is a perfect mirror reflecting what is, *as it is*. To suppose the mind such a mirror, is obviously to take a metaphor for a fact. 'The human understanding' as one of the greatest thinkers finely said 'is like an *unequal* mirror to the rays of things, *which, mixing its own nature with the nature of things, distorts and perverts them.*'[55]

A similar phrase on taking a metaphor for a fact is used in *Middlemarch* as the novelist considers the reason for 'a certain blankness of sensibility which came over' Mr Casaubon 'just when his expectant gladness should have been most lively'.

[He] had imagined that his long studious bachelorhood had stored up for him a compound interest of enjoyment, and that large drafts on his affections would not fail to be honoured; for we all of us, grave or light, get our thoughts entangled in metaphors, and act fatally on the strength of them. (Ch. 10)

If George Eliot feels that any correction is necessary in Spinoza's system as 'translated' for the novel-reader, it seems likely that she wishes to avoid any apparent overemphasis on the importance of 'active thought' as the groundwork of human relationships. Certainly there is no element of hardness or narrowness in the clarity of self-knowledge which Spinoza advocates, and in Dorothea, as the central character of the novel, 'active thought' is also 'vivid sympathetic experience'. It is of some interest however that we find among George Eliot's unpublished memoranda (first put into print in 1884) a note on 'the efficacy of feeling' and the 'impulse and act' of heroism and vain self-sacrifice, which ends with these words:

No doubt the passionate inspiration which prompts and sustains a course of self-sacrificing labour in the light of soberly estimated results gathers the highest title to our veneration and makes the supreme heroism. But the generous leap of impulse is needed too to swell the flood of sympathy in us beholders, that we may not fall completely under the mastery of calculation, which in its turn may fail of ends for want of energy got from ardour. We have need to keep the sluices open for possible influxes of the rarer sort. [56]

Such a 'generous leap of impulse' is shown in the imagery of *Middlemarch* when Mrs Bulstrode feels dart into her mind

the idea of some guilt in her husband— then, under the working of terror came the image of her husband exposed to disgrace—and then, after an instant of scorching shame in which she felt only the eyes of the world, with one leap of the heart she was at his side. . . . All this went on within her in a mere flash of time . . . (Ch. 74).

This 'imperfectly-taught woman, whose phrases and habits were an odd patchwork' and who needs to have her brother tell her all the circumstances of the scandal 'very inartificially, in slow fragments', has yet a loyal spirit within her; one whose mind is quite untrained to active thought, may yet act rightly through an inspired energy of feeling.

'Every limit is a beginning as well as an ending': it seems that in trying to consider some aspects of the imagery of *Middlemarch* which have not hitherto been very much studied, I end, where I began, on the very threshold of the subject. What is beyond doubt is that the subject itself has an interest not easily exhausted.

6

Criticism of the Novel

Contemporary Reception

W. J. HARVEY

The immediate success of *Middlemarch* may have been proportioned rather to the author's reputation than to its intrinsic merits. It certainly lacks the peculiar charm of the early work . . . she seems to be a little out of touch with the actual world, and to speak from a position of philosophical detachment which somehow exhibits her characters in a rather distorting light. For that reason *Middlemarch* seems to fall short of the great masterpieces which imply a closer contact with the world of realities and less preoccupation with certain speculative doctrines.

Leslie Stephen, *George Eliot* (1902)

To the reader who holds a large stretch of her early work in view it will become obvious that the mist of recollection gradually withdraws. It is not that her power diminishes for, to our thinking, it is at its highest in the mature *Middlemarch*, the magnificent book which with all its imperfections is one of the few English novels written for grown-up people.

Virginia Woolf, 'George Eliot'
The Times Literary Supplement (1919)

I HAVE, of course, wrenched my epigraphs from their contexts; nevertheless, these two judgments may symbolize the slow swing of taste from generation to generation. Leslie Stephen's book on George Eliot is good, but modern criticism has generally seconded the opinion of his daughter. Though we are nowadays commonly agreed that *Middlemarch* is George Eliot's master-piece, this verdict was slow to form. George Eliot's contemporaries were by no means unanimous though, as Stephen says, many of them were clearly swayed by her reputation. The various essays on her by Henry James, for example, reflect a real and not untypical irresolution about the relative merits of her novels. While the reviewer in *St Paul's Magazine* was safe in asserting that the critics 'all unite in regarding *Middlemarch* as one of the few great literary products of the generation', he could also point out that '*Romola* was the most frequently cited as her masterpiece, prior to the publication of *Middlemarch*'. Some critics remained loyal to this allegiance; thus the *London Quarterly Review* thought that '*Middlemarch* is perhaps more of a masterpiece than any work from the same hand except *Romola*'. Other reviewers differed, preferring 'the peculiar charm of the early work'. Thus the *Quarterly Review* maintains that *Adam Bede* is 'still by so many persons reckoned her masterpiece'. *The Times* reviewer certainly thought so; *Middlemarch*, compared with *Adam Bede*, 'as a novel proper . . . is inferior to the earlier work; its plot is not exciting; it has not the liveliness, variety and picturesqueness of its great predecessor'. Indeed, practically all her novels—excepting *Felix Holt*—had their particular champions; later, some reviewers saw even *Daniel Deronda* as the summit of George Eliot's achievement.

After nearly a century, then, the original diversity of critical opinion has gradually resolved into a remarkable unanimity. I do not propose to trace this process by attempting a full history of critical opinion; rather, I am concerned with the novel's immediate reception. Even here I shall be selective rather than inclusive, basing my comments on the evidence of twenty or so reviews which are, I think, reasonably typical of the range of contemporary opinion.[1] In examining these I shall try always to keep in mind the consensus of modern opinion since the publication of F. R. Leavis's *The Great Tradition*, Virginia Woolf's comment being proleptic rather than typical of her generation. In taking modern opinion as a point of reference, I shall be concerned not merely to discuss the different emphases, methods and assumptions of George Eliot's reviewers, but particularly to discover whether there remains anything valuable or viable for modern taste in the reviews, whether any points were stressed that nowadays we tend to overlook and whether there is any bias in modern criticism that may need correction. Equally, of course, there were various biases determining the nature of the contemporary reviews of *Middlemarch* and discovering these will, no doubt, throw some light on the history of taste and on the relative standards of reviewing then and now.

We may first isolate and briefly discuss one kind of critical approach available only to George Eliot's contemporaries; those reviews—for example, in the *Examiner*, the *Spectator* and the *Athenaeum*—which are a kind of serial response to the part-issue of *Middlemarch*. Lacking the knowledge of the novel's genesis which modern readers owe to Professors Kitchel and Beaty, contemporary reviewers saw the part issue of *Middlemarch* simply as a convenient mode of publication rather than as having any profound effect on the novel's design. Thus the *Athenaeum* (1 July 1872) declared that 'however *Middlemarch* may appear, it is clear that it has not been written, although published, serially', and this opinion was echoed by the *Spectator* (7 December 1872) which commented that George Eliot had clearly completed *Middlemarch* before starting to publish, since 'there is no sign of a half-complete or altered design anywhere'. The *Examiner* (2 December 1871), thinking like most of its contemporaries that plot-making is of relatively little importance in George Eliot's work, considered that *Middlemarch* would bear part-issue better than most novels; while the reader might feel irritated at first he would eventually gain by the slow and careful reading thus imposed upon him. Later (20 March 1872) it offered supporting evidence for this point of view: 'we heard the other day of a husband and wife who find in each two-monthly installment as much as they can read in the next two months, two or three pages affording the text for a whole evening's thought and discussion'—a convenient but, one would have thought, extreme instance of Victorian reading habits! Nevertheless, the *Examiner* had some faults to find in the part-issue structure. Of Book I it says (2 December 1871) :'The volume ends abruptly, and without any stage-appliances for bringing its characters into a focus, and concentrating the interest that has to be held in abeyance until the next installment is provided, and this arrangement is, perhaps, somewhat inartistic.'[2] Similarly, the *Athenaeum* (30 March 1872) thought that 'the third install-ment of *Middlemarch* ends in doubt—a doubt too evidently adapted to the exigencies of a serial form'. But such criticisms were few; most reviewers of the part-issues contented themselves with plot-paraphrases, character-sketches and general praise. These notices are, however, of particular interest in illustrating the conventional expectations to which George Eliot had suc-cumbed in *Adam Bede* and which she was to disappoint in *Middlemarch*. The *Edinburgh Review*, in discussing how part publication affected the novel's form, summed the matter up:

Each volume, up to the very last, left open the question whether the real hero and the real heroine of the book could not by some means be brought together, and we are not sure that the disappointment of the failure of this expectation will be easily got over.

This hope of a conventionally happy ending is most naïvely and consistently expressed in the *Examiner*. Of Book II of *Middle-march* the reviewer writes (3 February 1872):

If we were to attempt to forecast Dorothea's future, we should be inclined, we confess, to attach more importance to what we are told about Mr Lydgate, a young doctor, who has come to settle in Middle-march for a time, than to anything we learn relating directly to herself. There is obviously an artistic relationship already in course of being established between the two characters, and we fear this bodes no good to Dorothea.

What the reviewer means by 'an artistic relationship' becomes, alas, only too clear in his subsequent notices. Of Dorothea's marital disillusionment in Book III he writes (30 March 1872), 'the danger of mischief from her acquaintanceship with Mr Lydgate is increasing'. With Book IV (8 June 1872) he begins to have doubts: 'if Lydgate is to be brought into near relations with Dorothea, they are still far from one another'. Yet as the plot thickens in Book V (27 July 1872), 'it is not yet clear whether Ladislaw or Lydgate is to have most to do with her future life', while in Book VI (5 October 1872) Lydgate still appears to the

128

reviewer a possible alternative to Ladislaw. No one, he says, would regret Rosamond's death 'if thereby the clever man and the refined woman of the novel were to be brought into closer relations'. Even in his review of *Middlemarch* as a whole (7 December 1872) it is obviously only with great reluctance that he acquiesces in George Eliot's completed design:

If we part from Dorothea with some regret that her first great failure, as the wife of Mr Casaubon, should have no better compensation than the very prosaic success of a marriage with Will Ladislaw, it is doubtless only just such a regret as the author wishes to arouse in us, as part of the regret with which every wise student must regard the accumulation of blunders and failure that too often befall the worthiest natures.

The attitude of this reviewer is important, not merely because he doubtless reflects the expectations of many of George Eliot's readers, but more particularly because it helps to determine his attitude to Ladislaw who is clearly the centre of much critical debate, both then and now. 'It is not easy', he writes in his general review, 'to like young Ladislaw; one is tempted to think that, in marrying him, Dorothea makes nearly as great a blunder as she did in marrying Mr Casaubon.' As we shall see later, many other critics also succumbed to this temptation and if they produce more sophisticated reasons for thinking Ladislaw an artistic failure, we should also remember that a frustrated taste for romantic endings based on popular notions of the proper roles of hero and heroine in fiction was also—and probably still is for many readers—a powerful factor in the formation of such critical judgments.

2

A major problem confronting both contemporary reviewers and modern critics is the adequate definition of the novel's subject, the correct location of its thematic centre. The question is well posed in the *Atlantic Monthly*, whose critic finds the sub-title less than helpful:

It is, says one critic, the study of the effects of the narrow English provincial life of forty years ago on the characters of the story which interests the author, and therefore should interest the readers. If this is so, we say that, somehow or other, the effects of this narrow provincial life on the characters is the last thing in the world we should have supposed the central point of interest. . . . Someone else says that it is Dorothea's life which is the main thing; the struggle of an ardent, impassioned and noble nature with surrounding obstacles. . . . But though there is certainly some reason for this opinion, there is just as much for the opinion that Lydgate is the central figure.

We may notice here one possible source of confusion; namely, the tendency (illustrated in the previous section) to think of a novel's subject strictly in terms of its hero and heroine. Most reviewers are content to grant Lydgate and Dorothea this conventional status though, in terms of the attention paid to him, Lydgate appears only a subordinate figure to the critics of *Blackwood's* and *St Paul's Magazine*. In other journals (the *Examiner*, for instance) attention is concentrated mainly on the heroine, possibly because an undue emphasis is given to the Prelude of *Middlemarch*. Henry James, in the *Galaxy*, for example, appears to think that George Eliot intended a detailed study of a central figure, Dorothea *en disponsibilité*, only to be diverted by her lack of artistic control into a panoramic study of society. *The Times*, as one might expect, sits comfortably on the fence; while it allows that the Prelude and Finale 'seem to give the clue of a purpose, not obtrusively put forward in the body of the story', it insists that the work is not concentrated to one point; 'its variety and interest are not subordinated to a single meaning' embodied in Dorothea. Still other critics stress the Prelude but see it as foreshadowing a general and not a personal theme.

Very roughly we may say that the location of the theme lies between two extremes, neither of which is asserted in a wholly pure state by any critic. One extreme would see the novel's subject as essentially psychological or spiritual; concerned, that is to say, with the internal consciousness and development of a few characters confronted with particular moral problems and not meant to typify any general social or philosophical doctrine. The *Academy* comes, perhaps, closest to this position. It begins by firmly asserting that:

Middlemarch marks an epoch in the history of fiction in so far as its incidents are taken from the inner life, as the action is developed by the direct influence of mind on mind and character on character, as the material circumstances of the outer world are made subordinate and accessory to the artistic presentation of a definite passage of mental experience, but chiefly as giving a background of perfect realistic truth to a profoundly imaginative psychological study.

While the realism of George Eliot's social analysis is recognized and praised, yet the 'complicated conditions of so seemingly simple a thing as provincial life are not the main subject of the work'. It only forms

the background of relief to two or three spiritual conflicts, the scenery amongst which two or three souls spend some eventful years in working out their own salvation and their neighbours', or in effecting, with equal labour, something less than salvation for both. The story of these conflicts and struggles is the thread which unites the whole.

Confronted with the deterministic aspects of the book the *Academy* counters with a quotation which was obviously a favourite of many reviewers: 'It always remains true that if we had been greater, circumstances would have been less strong against us.' Clearly such a critic had to come to terms with the deterministic qualities of the book, since these would naturally be emphasized by advocates of the opposing extreme. This point of view would understand the novel to be concerned with society rather than with the individual, since it would see the thematic centre as lying in the effects of environment and would stress the characters as examples of social frustration. A particular variant of this view conceives Dorothea as typifying the 'Woman Question' and in general the emphasis of this approach is on some such abstract theme or problem. The *Athenaeum* (7 December 1872) perhaps comes closest to a bald statement of this view; detecting a Comtist keynote in *Middlemarch*, it thinks that the novel's purpose is to show 'that in an organized society where each of us finds his place, mistakes such as those of Dorothea and Lydgate would be impossible, or, at any rate, less sadly possible, than they are now'.

Other contemporary reviews might seem at first to endorse an abstract theme. As the *Atlantic Monthly* observes:

Several critics have agreed, and it is almost becoming the fashion to say, that the leading trait in all of George Eliot's works is the constant presence of the idea of Fate or Destiny, of the helplessness of man in his pitiful attempt to struggle with the eternal forces of nature.

But as the reviewer is careful to point out:

The idea of fate is very different in different minds, and it seems to us by no means clear that the fate of George Eliot is of a sort which has hitherto been known to literature. . . . Hers is a more modern and truer conception. The destiny which surrounds her characters . . . is the compounded description of natural laws, character, and accident which we call life. It leaves nothing out of view; neither the material nor the moral forces; neither the immutable fixity of physical succession, nor the will. Man is, in these novels, neither a creature who controls . . . nor who is controlled by nature; he is himself part of nature.

Most reviewers were, in fact, much too responsive and sophisticated to adopt this extreme position; some of them (for example, the *Spectator*, 7 December 1872) explicitly state that the 'Woman Question' is an inadequate formulation of the novel's theme. Most of them, like most modern critics, were content to see the truth as lying between these two extremes and to define the novel's theme in terms of a balance or a tension between individual characterization and social analysis. The question then becomes—what, precisely, *is* the balance struck by George Eliot? The problem is treated sensibly by most Victorian critics, but no more intelligent treatment is to be found than in the *British Quarterly Review*. At first the reviewer seems to veer to an extreme position:

Middlemarch is, as the preface . . . pretty plainly confesses, a sort of pictorial indictment of modern society for the crippling conditions it imposes on men and women, especially women, of high ideal enthusiasm.

But he soon qualifies this viewpoint; because George Eliot's theme is the paralysis of noble natures:

it was essential for her to give such a solidity and complexity to her picture of the world by which her hero's and heroine's idealism was to be more or less tested, and partly subjugated, as would justify the impression that she understood fully the character of the struggle.

Pursuing this theme leads him to an interesting insight which, so far as I know, has been generally overlooked by modern critics, no doubt because the crux occurs only in the first edition of *Middlemarch*. It seems to me very probable that its subsequent deletion is George Eliot's response to the verdict of her reviewers. The crucial passage occurs in the Finale, where George Eliot writes of Dorothea:

Certainly those determining acts of her life were not ideally beautiful. They were the mixed result of young and noble impulse struggling under prosaic conditions. Among the many remarks passed on her mistakes, it was never said in the neighbourhood of Middlemarch that such mistakes could not have happened if the society into which she was born had not smiled on propositions of marriage from a sickly man to a girl less than half his own age, on modes of education which make a woman's knowledge another name for motley ignorance, on rules of conduct which are in flat contradiction with its own loudly-asserted beliefs.[3]

The reviewers really pounced on this passage; the *British Quarterly Review* was moderate when it observed that this comment

really has no foundation at all in the tale itself. . . . We hardly see how Dorothea could have been better protected against her first mistake than the picture of social life in Middlemarch represents her as actually having been protected . . . we find in this passage a trace that George Eliot is, on reviewing her own work, a little dissatisfied with her own picture of the 'prosaic conditions' to which she ascribes Dorothea's misadventures; and that she tries to persuade herself that they were actually more oppressive and paralyzing than they really were. It is obvious, we think, that Dorothea's character was one of much more impetuous self-assertion, of much more adventurous and self-willed idealism than this passage would suggest. . . . George Eliot is hardly fair to the society she has herself so wonderfully portrayed, when she throws the responsibility of Dorothea's first great mistake upon it.

The same criticism is made, often more sharply, by the *North American Review*, the *Spectator* (7 December 1872), the *Athenaeum*

(7 December 1872) and *The Times*. Only the *Examiner* quotes the crucial passage without perceiving the contradiction between the narrative and the omniscient assertion; only the *Fortnightly Review* attempts to defend George Eliot. While it agrees that Dorothea does not yield to social pressures in marrying Casaubon, but is simply deluded about him, it argues that George Eliot shows that 'it is society which so nurtured women that their ideals cannot but be ideals of delusion'. While it finds that the Prelude and Finale are in themselves ambiguous on this point it pleads that there are 'certainly passages enough in the body of the narrative which point the same remonstrance against what society does for women'. The reviewer conveniently ignores the fact that there are other women in this society—for example, Celia and Mary Garth—who are *not* so deluded. The reviewers, then, were certainly lynx-eyed on points of detail, however uncertain they were as to the general thematic direction of the book. On this matter, I feel, modern critics can hardly pretend to much superiority; a reading of recent criticism would reveal much the same range of opinion and variety of emphasis.

3

Consideration of theme leads naturally to consideration of structure. 'It is a treasure house of detail but it is an indifferent whole', wrote Henry James in his *Galaxy* review. A great deal of modern criticism has been devoted to defending *Middlemarch* against James's judgment by attempting to analyse the structural principles which unify and discipline the multifarious interests of the novel. If anything, the novel is now in danger of seeming oppressively over-organized as one pattern, one imaginative configuration after another, is laid bare for our inspection by the tools of critical analysis. Few contemporary reviewers would have understood or shared this concern. Occasionally one finds a flat, unsupported assertion of the novel's structural integrity:

Each chapter of the story has been written with every other chapter in view, each fitting into each as exactly as the pieces in some elaborate Chinese puzzle. (*Saturday Review*, 7 December 1872)

But this is rare; most reviewers are content simply to catalogue various choice items in the 'treasure house of detail'. One reason for this may be that most contemporary critics would have equated structure with plot and all were agreed that plot is not the most important thing about *Middlemarch*. True, they find particular flaws. When Henry James writes:

To but one of the accessory episodes—that of Mr Bulstrode, with its multiplex ramifications, do we take exception. It has a slightly artificial cast, a melodramatic tinge, unfriendly to the richly natural colouring of the whole. Bulstrode himself—with the history of whose troubled conscience the author has taken great pains—is, to our sense, diffusely treated; he never grasps the reader's attention. . . .

he would have found at least partial support among his fellow reviewers. None of them would have supported his aberrant judgment on Bulstrode's character; like most modern critics they concurred in thinking this one of the novel's triumphs. But they would have agreed about the 'multiplex ramifications'; James is echoed by *The Times*: 'The mysteries about Ladislaw's ancestry and Bulstrode's antecedents may have a mean and commonplace effect against the rich texture of better matters.'

The *Fortnightly Review* also notes this as one of a number of minor flaws in the plot. But for most reviewers character is everything. Thus the *Saturday Review* (21 December 1872) doubts if Casaubon or Bulstrode, *as they affect the plot*, are particularly effective; but this does not matter, says the reviewer, since we appreciate them for what they are in themselves. The *Edinburgh Review* agrees, with only a slight qualification:

To most readers the figure of the religious and criminal Banker will appear the most forcible portion of the story. It has, however, little real bearing on any of the three groups of characters, but touches each of them with sufficient art not to seem intrusive.

To describe in detail this delight in character would be tedious and unnecessary. Much of it is expressed naively in long character sketches which are generally alien to modern taste and critical practice. Sometimes one notes a view too easily assumed or established to satisfy the modern critic's thirst for complexity:

The reader soon has for himself, thanks to George Eliot's care and tact, no doubts about Dorothea. The easy but consummate skill, with which the heroine is put in the right light, can hardly be overpraised. (*Quarterly Review*)

Sometimes one applauds the fine statement of just perception; thus Casaubon:

acts upon Dorothea as a mere moral sponge. . . . The picture is, and is meant to be, one of moral *waste*, of a rich and generous and buoyant nature wasted on one who was only rendered restless and exhausted by intercourse with her. (*British Quarterly Review*)

But there is little value in trying to sum up the debits and credits of Victorian character appreciation. I wish, rather, to isolate three points for particular comment.

First, there is the obvious relish displayed for the minor characters of the book: Mrs Cadwallader and Brooke, Farebrother and Caleb Garth, Trumbull and Featherstone—all the lesser figures are clearly enjoyed and frequently occupy as much of the reviewer's space as the major characters. If *Middlemarch* is panoramic, then its landscape is densely populated and to this abundance the Victorians responded. In this, I suspect, they approximate more closely than many modern critics to the experience of the common reader. Perhaps—though I am probably stretching this view to the point of caricature—after a generation of depth psychology, interior monologues, alienated heroes and heroines of exquisite sensibility, we are only just beginning to respond naturally again to a buzzing, crowded, cluttered fictional world.

Second, one notices that the reviewers are not afraid to deploy canons of verisimilitude, often in a blunt and downright manner. They are not afraid of asking the simple question, 'Is this true to life?' and of giving simple answers. Again, I suspect that much modern criticism, in its emphasis on technical analysis, ignores or evades this question. Thus the *Spectator* (7 December 1872) thinks Bulstrode a successful character, but:

We cannot help thinking that George Eliot makes a mistake in representing a man of Bulstrode's type of mind as entirely unoppressed by the guilt of what he well knew to be, morally, murder, until disgrace comes upon him. The description of the crime itself is wonderfully fine; but the complete equanimity with which he looks back upon it, after the great struggle which preceded it, we cannot accept as true.

We may think this particular comment just or unjust; but the point is, that we rarely meet with this *type* of comment in modern criticism. Perhaps we are simply less confident of where the truth in life lies. We stress too much, perhaps, the functional or structural aspects of character and too little relish characters as ends-in-themselves. Perhaps we are afraid of the 'portrait-gallery' type of criticism; perhaps we assume the primacy of simple enjoyment as a datum not worth discussing; perhaps we have been too heavily dosed with 'moral seriousness'—though here, as we shall see, we can hardly compete with Victorians.

The last point to notice is that the Victorians *do* see the connections between character and total structure. Sometimes their perceptions are so fragmentary, so casually expressed or so tangential to their argument that one is left unsure as to how sophisticated or self-aware they really are. When, for example, the *Quarterly Review* asks the reader 'to realize the consistent patience and infinite pains with which our authoress works' he quotes, conventionally enough, a number of small, isolated but striking, scenes and descriptions. But then he continues: 'Or again, let the juxtapositions and oppositions of character be considered. Take the slight sketch of Mr and Mrs Cadwallader . . . or take, on a larger scale, the surroundings of Ladislaw and Lydgate.' Is the reviewer unconscious of the full implications for the structure of the novel of his remark, or does he take them so much for granted as not to need detailed consideration? One guesses the former—but it is only a guess.

Sometimes remarks involving both character and structure are rudimentary but clear enough. Dowden, in the second of his *Contemporary Review* essays, sees the Prelude to *Middlemarch* as setting forth the main theme, but as applying to both Dorothea and Lydgate; 'Heart and brain prove alike failures'. The simplicity of this had already been sophisticated in the *Academy*:

Unlike most of the other characters, Lydgate does not become thoroughly intelligible till the last number of the work has been read in connection with the first: then he appears as a masculine counterpart to Dorothea with the relative proportions of head and heart reversed.

The same point is part of the most interesting passage of an otherwise unremarkable *critique* in the *London Quarterly Review*. The reviewer has been analysing Bulstrode at some length:

We have dwelt more particularly on this man's character and career, not because he is one of the principal characters in the drama of Middlemarch life, regarded from an artistic point of view, but because all that relates to him is of vital interest to every serious-minded person, and it is not so difficult to separate from the book as some portions of greater beauty and more artistic importance. He is also a factor of some consequence in the destinies of several characters intrinsicially more important—notably of the two chief personages, Dorothea and Lydgate; and he is an integer in the triply-embodied conception of the futility of exclusively self-seeking efforts. Peter Featherstone, with his property in land and funds, and his desire to show his power in disposing of the same; Casaubon, with his inordinate vanity, that will sacrifice all to his worthless book and his unreasonable jealousy and suspicion; and Bulstrode, with his insatiable desire to appear as a shining light before all men, are all frustrated through that narrow-minded egoism that has no eye for the inexorable influences of external circumstance. What may perhaps be regarded as the main conception of the book, is embodied in the two characters that we have already pointed out as the chief personages, Dorothea and Lydgate, whom we may perhaps venture to designate as psychological correlates. . . .

This passage is worth examining in some detail. It is not merely that the last sentence hints at a greater depth of perception than is shown elsewhere in the review. There is also the curious near-contradiction between the first and the second sentences. Bulstrode is nominally chosen because he is easily detachable from the novel; yet the reviewer immediately asserts, with admirable shrewdness and economy, precisely those ways in which he *cannot* be so detached, and gives us a fine though incomplete analysis of Bulstrode's role in the total structure of *Middlemarch*. We should remember that the work of Victorian reviewers, no less than that of Victorian novelists, was determined by the nature of their medium and the expectations of their reading public. No doubt the easiest way to fill out a long review is to detach characters and create a 'portrait-gallery', or to give a plot-paraphrase amply padded with illustrative quotation. That applies to a great many reviews under consideration in this essay. But we should also remember the taste of *particular* reading publics subscribing to *particular* journals; this, no doubt, helped to shape the point and substance of particular reviews. In this instance, Bulstrode was chosen because 'all that relates to him is of vital interest to every serious-minded person'. The reviewer knew his audience; the *London Quarterly Review* was generally conservative in tone and religious in content; it was aimed chiefly at the Methodists. So it is no wonder that Bulstrode, the religious hypocrite with his roots in Evangelical Dissent, should have been isolated for particular emphasis.

In general, then, Victorian reviewers, while delighting naively in character creation, also show signs of a more sophisticated perception of character in relation to structure and theme. This is particularly true when we turn to an issue which has also occupied the attention of much modern criticism—the relation of the author herself to her fiction.

4

One of the main streams of modern criticism flows from its source in Edward Dowden's first *Contemporary Review* essay on George Eliot. There, perhaps because he knew that George Eliot's 'philosophy' was too gloomy or too non-religious for many of her readers, he made his famous distinction:

When we have passed in review the works of that great writer who calls herself George Eliot, and given for a time our use of sight to the portraitures of men and women, what form, as we move away, persists on the field of vision, and remains the chief centre of interest for the imagination? The form not of Tito, or Maggie, or Dinah, or Silas, but of one who, if not the real George Eliot, is that 'second self' who writes her books, and lives and speaks through them. Such a second self of an author is perhaps more substantial than any mere human personality encumbered with the accidents of flesh and blood and daily living. It stands at some distance from the primary self, and differs considerably from its fellow. It presents its person to us with fewer reserves; it is independent of local and temporary motives of speech or of silence; it knows no man after the flesh; it is more than an individual; it utters secrets, but secrets which all men of all ages are to catch; while behind it, lurks well pleased the veritable historical self secure from impertinent observation and criticism.

Dowden stood alone in this distinction between the author's 'second self' and her 'veritable historical self'. His fellow reviewers simply equated the omniscient voice of the novels with George Eliot and in their simplicity I concur, fruitful though Dowden's distinction has subsequently become. For most of her reviewers, as for many modern critics, this omniscient control is at once a source of strength and weakness. From it stems the moral earnestness, intensity and complexity to which they so fervently respond; yet it makes them uncomfortable. The *Edinburgh Review* concedes that George Eliot's observations and reflections are inserted 'opportunely' into *Middlemarch*, yet

Strictly speaking, the writer should be as little seen in person in a novel as he would be in a modern drama, where he only gives the stage directions; but here the Chorus is too continually present, calling us away from the excitement and anxiety of the piece to the consideration of the external moralities and humorous contrasts of life.

For the *Atlantic Monthly*, sometimes the characters

are, after all, only masks through which George Eliot is ventriloquizing. . . . Though their psychological situations are always interesting, they seem always to be doing the work of representation for man or woman—not that they are types, but that their movements seem a trifle too much in the control of the wonderful exhibitor who is half concealed behind the show.

The general view is summed up by the *Spectator* (5 October 1872):

What gives a great deal of their peculiar stamp, both in the way of fresh interest, and of questionable or even challengeable drift, to George Eliot's pictures, is the theoretic nature of the moral anatomy which she applies to her own creations, subtle and wonderful as its range certainly is. She has a speculative philosophy of character that always runs on in a parallel stream with her picture of character, sometimes adding to it an extraordinary fascination, sometimes seeming to distort it by a vein of needless and perhaps unjust suggestion. Her characters are so real that they have a life and body of their own quite distinct from her criticism of them; and one is conscious at times of taking part with the characters against the author, and of accusing her of availing herself unfairly of the privilege of author, by adding a trait that bears out her own *criticism* rather than her own imaginative conception.

The *Spectator* here elaborates a point which it had already mentioned in its review of Book III of *Middlemarch* (30 March 1872) where it maintains that we sometimes suspect

the author's impartiality. . . . It is Thackeray who has set the example which George Eliot so freely follows of playing unfeeling critic to his own creations, but Thackeray is at least pretty impartial, and criticizes his 'puppets' all round with even satiric indifference. George Eliot has favourites and aversions, and deals hardly with the latter.

The example given is the contrasting treatment of Rosamond and Celia, an instance also cited by the *Fortnightly Review*. But clearly the crucial case is George Eliot's treatment of Will Ladislaw.

Most modern critics agree that George Eliot fails in her treatment of Ladislaw; so do most Victorian reviewers. But the grounds of disappointment differ. Nowadays most of us, I suppose, would say something to the effect that in Ladislaw George Eliot asserts more than she demonstrates, that she loads him with a value which as an imagined human being he cannot possibly bear. Some of us would link this to a limitation in George Eliot's ability to deal with certain sectors of human experience; in *Middlemarch* we expect, perhaps, the pattern of *The Bostonians* and are disappointed when we don't find it. That is to say, after the vividly imagined failure in the marriage relationship of Dorothea and Casaubon, we look for a compensating embodiment of human love, romantic love, sexual passion. Naturally enough, the Victorian reviewers say nothing of George Eliot's failure to dramatize this area of experience. Many of them, like the *Edinburgh Review*, are quite willing to accept at their face value the love scenes between Dorothea and

Ladislaw. With them, it is rather the disappointment at discerning a *moral* inadequacy; what they feel is the disproportion between the high ideals and spiritual ardour of Dorothea and the commonplace nature of the young man she squanders herself on. With this is linked a sense of intrusive bias; Ladislaw is George Eliot's pet, her spoiled darling. One illustration must stand for all; I quote the lively acerbity of the *Saturday Review* which considers Dorothea's second choice of a husband banal, 'the ball-room choice of any ordinary girl':

There are two views of Ladislaw who, we scarcely know on what reasonable grounds, is a great favourite with the author. . . . He does what he likes, whether right or wrong, to the end of the story; he makes no sacrifices; even his devotion to Dorothea does not preserve him from an unworthy flirtation with his friend Lydgate's wife. . . . Poor Lydgate—ten times the better man—suffers not only in happiness, but in his noblest ambitions, and sinks to the level of a good practice and a good income because he marries and is faithful to the vain selfish creature whom Ladislaw merely flirts with.

What is interesting is that the range of Victorian response is rather more varied and complicated than that of modern criticism. Some reviewers are simply disappointed. Some—like the *North American Review*—find George Eliot's treatment of Ladislaw ambiguous.

As to the other marriage with Ladislaw, it is not easy to make out the author's opinion, whether it is one of approval or disapprobation. The same obscurity exists with regard to Ladislaw himself, who seems to be a favourite with the writer to an extent which hardly justifies itself to the mind of the reader.

For three reviewers, at least, the anti-climax of Ladislaw is seen as deliberate and intentional, as working out the Saint Theresa theme to the very end. Thus the *British Quarterly Review* cannot view Dorothea's marriage to Ladislaw as

a moral compensation. . . . She lavishes herself on Will Ladislaw as a sort of generous compensation for his relation's coldness to him; and one feels, and is probably meant to feel acutely, that here, too, it is 'the meanness of opportunity' and not intrinsic suitability, which determines Dorothea's second comparatively happy marriage.

Thus the *Fortnightly Review*:

> We have been made to feel all along that he is hardly worthy of her. There is no sense of triumph in it; there is rather a sense of sadness in a subdued and restricted, if not a thwarted destiny.

A similar opinion is also implicit in the passage in the *Examiner* (quoted in Section I) on Dorothea's second marriage. It is a point of view well worth considering, and one, perhaps, that has been too little considered by modern critics.

5

The critics are nearly unanimous about Ladislaw; equally—and there is a clear link—they are nearly unanimous about the book's tone which derives for them from its prevailing moral temper. It is a sad, melancholy book. In no more striking way do Victorian reviewers differ from modern critics than in their primary concern for the book's 'message'. Equally they differ in the confidence with which they judge this 'message' by the standards of their own deepest beliefs. These standards and beliefs in general are, of course, Christian and most reviewers face squarely the fact that they are dealing with a profoundly moral but profoundly non-Christian work.[4]

We should not dismiss this concern with 'message' nor should we imagine that their firm application of Christian standards is done with anything but tact, sympathy and sensitivity. Their interest in the former leads them to the true perception and fine statement of qualities which are clearly part of the novel's strength. Thus, for example, the *London Quarterly Review*:

> It is not in what is called the 'plot' of her books that one discerns the strength and weight of George Eliot's intellect or the wealth of her imagination; the latter is always most notable in the solidity and completeness of her characters, the former in her wide and deep scientific knowledge, her absolute insight into the significance of everyday things, and that keen vision of the links in the chain of common circumstance whereby the most trivial act seems to become in her books the aperture through which she sweeps down a vista of constantly accumulating results.

And, similarly, *The Times*:

Nothing can more resemble the course of life than the manner in which the various persons have at first their separate existences, but are gradually thrown together, their lives, like different streams, falling into the river of the story as it flows to the sea.

As for their standards, these reviewers are the opposite of crudely ideological. They are full of sympathy, tolerance, understanding, praise. Their ultimate criteria operate only in the last analysis—which is just as it should be. But in the last analysis, when comparing *Middlemarch* with the very greatest works of art, many of these critics find something lacking and this they ascribe to George Eliot's lack of faith. In our more secular age we should probably ascribe it to a limitation in the range of *human* experience available to her imagination; we might say that while she has many of the Tolstoyan virtues she lacks something of Tolstoy's scope and intensity. But for the Victorian reviewer human experience is topped and completed by a sense of the divine, and this is a viewpoint worthy of respect if only because its results in terms of criticism are so striking. Consider one particular case; the *Spectator* (7 December 1872) points out that many of her characters are religious in temperament:

but in all these cases the province chosen for the religious temperament is solely the discharge of moral duty, and the side of these minds turned towards the divine centre of life is conspicuous only by its absence, especially in Dorothea's case. In reading the description of the night of Dorothea's darkest trial one feels a positive sense of vacancy; so dramatic a picture of such a one as she is, going through such a struggle without a thought of God, is really unnatural.

We may, nowadays, not react to the scene in quite the same way; nevertheless this seems to me substantial criticism and entirely fair comment. Indeed much of the strength and energy of these reviews derives from the tension between the impulse towards imaginative acceptance of George Eliot's world and the impulse towards final judgments based on personal convictions. As evidence of this I would cite the whole of the fine essay in the

British Quarterly Review with its striking and, indeed, moving conclusion.

George Eliot means to draw noble natures struggling hard against the currents of a poor kind of world, and without any trust in any invisible rock higher than themselves to which they can entreat to be lifted up. Such a picture is melancholy in its very conception. That in spite of this absence of any inward vista of spiritual hope, and in spite of the equally complete absence of any outward vista of 'far-resonant action', George Eliot should paint the noble characters in which her interest centres as clinging tenaciously to that *caput mortuum* into which Mr Arnold has so strangely reduced the Christian idea of God—'a stream of tendency, not ourselves, which makes for righteousness'—and as never inclined to cry out 'let us eat and drink, for tomorrow we die', is a great testimony to the ethical depth and purity of her mind. And it will add to the interest of *Middlemarch* in future generations, when at length this great wave of scepticism has swept by us, and 'this tyranny is overpast', that in pointing to it as registering the low tide-mark of spiritual belief among the literary class in the nineteenth-century, the critics of the future will be compelled to infer from it, that even during that low ebb of trust in the supernatural element of religion, there was no want of ardent belief in the spiritual obligations of purity and self-sacrifice, nor even in that 'secret of the Cross' which, strangely enough, survives the loss of the faith from which it sprung.

6

The first thing that struck me when making this survey of the contemporary reception of *Middlemarch*—and will, no doubt, have struck the reader who has survived thus far—is its sheer quantity. More than a hundred thousand words of comment formed the subject of this essay; had I attempted a fully comprehensive study of all the reviews, this figure would probably have doubled. Nowadays no writer, however great, would command such immediately profuse attention. The only remotely comparable instances in modern fiction have been the publication of *Dr Zhivago* and *Lady Chatterley's Lover*—and clearly, very special reasons operated in both these cases. But equally impressive has been the general quality of the reviews, the consistent seriousness of attention and concern.

In working towards a conclusion, I shall not try to measure Victorian achievement against modern achievement; I do not want to count gains and losses. Certain differences are, however, evident. Nowadays, most modern criticism is based, more or less directly, on a conception of aesthetic unity. This we owe largely to the work of Henry James and only his *Galaxy* review, among all the reviews, really foreshadows this. Much thereby has been gained. But perhaps, as a result, we respond less readily than the Victorians to local felicities, we are less able to enjoy a panorama as being merely panoramic, we are relatively ill at ease in the presence of a 'loose, baggy monster'—not that *Middlemarch* is *that*. Because of our concern with unity we are perhaps less well equipped to appreciate fictional characters in and for themselves. Though for the Victorians *Middlemarch* was a profoundly melancholy book, perhaps they enjoyed the range and variety of its humour more than we do. On the other hand, techniques of close analysis enable us to deal more adequately with the texture of the work; the reviewers' remarks on style are generally brief, perfunctory and conventional, while the idea of a significant 'pattern of images' would have seemed strange to them.

One further point about the Victorian reviewers needs to be mentioned. This is how often they display a striking historical self-consciousness, an awareness of themselves as incapsulated in a particular epoch, but with a strong sense of the continuum of before and after. This was clearly of immense help when dealing with a nearly-historical novel like *Middlemarch*. Thus the reviewer in *Blackwood's Magazine* saw clearly enough what we have only recently begun to see again: 'Though the story dates back to the days of Mr Peel and the Catholic Question, we see some of the political and social problems of our own times casting their shadows before them, and they are evidently present in the author's mind.'

It comes out, in a different way, in the *Quarterly Review*:

George Eliot follows, though dwarfed and darkened by the long shadow of her predecessor, in the wake of Walter Scott, and has the same happy fortune with him to be able readily to link the present to the past. Possibly the life of England is changing, perhaps has already changed, far more than we realise. The growth of enormous cities, the ease of travelling and the taste for travelling, the largeness and organisation of commercial and industrial energy, the disappearance of those local attachments and local peculiarities, which used to hold us so strongly because they had bound our fathers and grandfathers before us —these imply, it may be, a more rapid transition from one state of national development to another than can be made clear to those in whose unconscious presence the process has accomplished itself. . . . There is about books, such as those of George Eliot, much to make one ponder whether the course of the English novel may not be well-nigh run. . . . It appears as if, in Europe, we had reached the highest point of excellence in the development of a prose imaginative literature. Already the finest creative fancy begins to turn into other ways. How much suppressed imagination which, a while ago, would have sought expression in works of fiction, is traceable in the investigations, which gain moreover an ever-increasing popularity, into the problems of ancient law, of primitive society, and of natural history. . . .

Such remarks may seem strikingly modern, but we should learn from the spirit behind them and match the Victorians with our own historical awareness. We should value their criticism because it is theirs and not because it foreshadows our own interests and points of view; we should seek from them not confirmation but a sense of difference. And we should hope that our critical achievement in the field of literary reviewing will stand the test of time as well as theirs has stood it.

7

The Surface of the Novel

Chapter 30

BARBARA HARDY

THE whole has undoubtedly had a better press than the part, 'unity' as William James observed in *Pragmatism*, 'being more illustrious than variety'. There is no need to labour our recent concern with unity in theoretical and analytical criticism, but what is perhaps slightly surprising is the neglect of parts and details even in Victorian criticism. Variety is appreciated, and details are mentioned, but in too random and unsystematic a way to throw light on the qualities of randomness itself. Henry James, the most sophisticated contemporary critic of *Middlemarch*, never really explained what he had in mind when he called it 'a treasure-house of detail'. He made it clear why he considered it 'an indifferent whole', but the detail he praised rather than appreciated. My concern in this essay is with the detail.

I start with the assumption, more easily accepted than acted upon in critical practice, that some details are more local and more superficial than others. The objects, events, and images in this treasure-house of detail are not all equally profound, micro-cosmic, or symbolic. Some details lie casually on the surface, taking their place in a rendering of people, feelings, places, and ideas, are more or less memorable, more or less connected with other details. The casualness may be true or deceptive: some very unnoticeable details come to pick up colour and resonance from connections and repetitions, some do not; some arresting images do not belong to an elaborate network of metaphor and symbol. When we first move over the surface of the novel we tend to be less observant of relative complexity. When we come at a later stage to analyse the novel we may tend to treat details too evenly and uniformly as epitome and symbol, as surface details sinking the same kind and size of shaft into depths of generalization and association. The locally simple detail is frequently ignored or distorted.

One of the disadvantages of the critical tendency to over-generalize is its remoteness from reading experience. The pre-occupation with the part as representative of the whole tends to back away from a fully responsive reading. In speaking of this kind of reading I should like to remain deliberately vague, hoping to include the experience of an unprofessional but sensitive and intelligent reader and a critic's more alert and distanced reading which has not passed quite beyond empathy into note-taking. The note-taking stage is, in my experience, particularly difficult in the novels of George Eliot. Even when searching or checking in a highly reductive way, to find images or phrases belonging to a series, I have found myself dragged back into an absorbed reading of the story and its characters, the analysis arrested. The same kind of reductive checking of similar details in Dickens and Meredith, for example, has been much easier and less interrupted, though the experience will obviously vary from critic to critic as well as from author to author.

This personal detail will perhaps serve to declare my own interest in structural analysis. It is in no anti-formal spirit that I set out to look at parts in their own right, not just as complex epitomes. I think it is indeed impossible to acknowledge the importance of local and simple effect without being interested in the total structure. Henry James said nothing of interest about the details in this treasure-house because he saw no figure in the carpet. Victorian criticism was fairly inept at appreciating wholes, and James was inept at appreciating wholes which did not resemble his own ideal of concentration and total relevance, so it is in fact only slightly surprising that neither part nor whole should have been properly discussed in nineteenth-century criticism. We have to perceive the structure of imagery in order to see what lies within the main series, what lies on the edge, and what seems to lie outside. I began with the intention of looking at the part rather than the organization but came to conclude that looking hard at the part also brings out other aspects of organization—the local configurations of scene and chapter which are also neglected in most structural analysis. I want to say that some parts are simple and not symbolic, but that other, larger units are more intricately and systematically organized than I had imagined. If we look hard at each detail in a particular chapter, for instance, we learn more about the structure of the chapter than if we simply hop from key image to key image, placing our details on the very large scaffolding of the novel 'as a whole'. It is with local form as well as with small detail that I am here concerned.

My starting-point was the small detail. It is plain, I imagine, to most readers of Samuel Beckett, that there are sources of narrative power which lie outside the scheme of formal analysis. Beckett constantly disturbs any search for unity by his intransigent and opaque particulars, which strike us violently as baffling, disconnected, mysterious, odd, leading nowhere or certainly not where we had expected. More conventional novelists also convey more through individual moments of sensation and feeling than we allow, not because they are driven to express despair, doubt, nihilism or absurdity, but in simple apprehension of the quality of individual experiences. The ways in which Victorian novelists convey particular sensations and feelings are more easily subsumed and more easily lost in an account of 'unity' or 'theme' than the ways of Beckett, but I have a strong feeling, composed of reverence and of irreverence, that most critics of earlier fiction could learn something from getting lost for a while in *Watt*. Reading Beckett is a good way of losing old bearings. If we are sufficiently moved by a detail or event without placing it in a pattern or progression it is a short step to being moved by the surface of detail even if it does take its place in a coherent pattern and conventional progression. It is necessary to appreciate *Middlemarch* 'superficially' as well as symbolically.

When we sit down and read a novel for the first time, it is, I suggest, with a feeling for local life. When we look up and verbalize our responses, it is 'this bit' that we appreciate, rather than structure and symbol. It is true, of course, that an atomized response is characteristic of unawareness, of impressionistic selection, and of incomplete understanding, but it seems to be also true that at mature stages of reading, there are some simple effects that remain simples and not part of a total 'gestalt', not at least in any tidy or obvious way. Those simples that are seen to become symbolically expressive are often reduced and hardened in critical analysis, the first vivid impact lost and discarded in the process of perceiving and restating generalization. Formal analysis tends to strip off surface in order to reveal symbol, and in so doing may give a stark and unreal account both of the art of the novelist and of the pleasure of the reader. In an appreciation of the conceptual and ordered pattern of events in *Middlemarch* we should be able to recognize that the symbolic pressure is made through particular feeling and sensation. When Dorothea returns to her disenchanted room, to see its furniture shrunken, its tapestry ghostly, its volumes of polite literature 'more like immovable imitations of books', the outside uniformly white in snow and uniformly low-hanging in cloud, it is plain that her emotional disenchantment on her wedding journey is taking a symbolic shape. What one should also acknowledge, I believe, is the sensational quality of the symbol. The visual and physical pressures are strong, in imagery like 'the unlit transparency' but also in the primary rendering of actual landscape and objects. It really is winter, and winter really is like this. The room's faded charm is its individual quality, not there for purposes of equation through metaphor. The scene is made particularly vivid by the subtle incorporation of objects that in fact lie outside the symbolic equation: it is easy enough to render desolation, disillusionment and emotional sterility through the uniform land and sky, through the faded tapestry, the pale stag, and the dull polite books, but the picture includes also 'the bright fire of dry oak-boughs burning on the dogs' and George Eliot, as elsewhere, makes her generalization by insisting on what will not translate into the appropriate emotional tones, and observes that the bright fire 'seemed an incongruous renewal of life and glow'. One can of course schematize even this effect by suggesting that the bright fire with its renewal of life and glow attaches itself to Dorothea, and represents her future renewal and her potential resilience. One might well hasten to attach the 'pale stag' to Casaubon, but the haste would be rash. When one actually reads the passage, what is important and conspicuous is the full acknowledgment of the appearances of the room. The physical impact, too, of Dorothea's presence, as she comes in, glowing from her toilet, can be symbolically related to imagery and action elsewhere, but is important as *particular* vitality. Her vitality is checked and chilled in this room, it is superfluous in these neutral surroundings and George Eliot makes us feel this. This account is, true, part of a so-called 'undramatic' author's commentary, and it is perhaps still essential to say that the materials of fiction should not be too crudely divided into commentary and drama. The commentary in this novel achieves much of its concreteness and vitality through sensation. The force of the general representation is inseparable from the sensuous feeling of this and other moments. George Eliot's symbols are effective in this way, rendered in the vitality of such individual moments. When Dorothea feels the impact of the red hangings in St Peter's 'like a disease of the retina', an image which is clearly related to major themes, situations, and other images, it is essential that we first recognize the pressure of the surface: *this* sight, *this* physical impact.

Once the dependence of symbol on particular sensation and feeling is admitted and described, it is easier to recognize and expect the unpurposive detail, whose effect is simply local and immediate. Structural criticism has to precede an analysis of detail, so that we can relax the effort to burrow below the surface, to generalize the particulars. The broad-meshed net is necessary but through it can escape the vitality and rhythm of actual response.

The innocent first reading is one in which we register ends rather than means. It moves from one impression to another, not in the big leaps of distanced analysis but in a continuous flow. Both the moments and the process too easily get forgotten. While we read we move through a continuum which is made up of many components, some emblematic, some simple, some transparent, some opaque, some arresting, some scarcely noticeable. Such a motion is less unlike the process of moving through an ordinary day's experience than formal analysis can afford to admit. A novel like *Middlemarch* makes sustained identification impossible, and ordinary egocentric living involves much observation and feeling of a vivid but detached kind. In life we are often on the fringe of personal involvement, responding to events, people and sensations in ways which can interrupt action, the dialogue of the mind with itself, and the streamy train of reverie. Much sensuous experience is not only fairly detached, but also fragmented and localized. Fiction offers us the inside of experience which is normally unavailable except in relation to ourselves, and it does so in a medium composed of a continuous but unpredictable set of stimulae. The continuum is certainly more ordered and lucid than the forms of actual living, but the most realistic fiction keeps some faith with the solid, discrete, and unpremeditated nature of actual experience through which we move while we wake. George Eliot presents the vivid impact of the present moment, and the process of *Middlemarch*, in authorial report and in dramatic scene, is a series of such moments, alive to sense and feeling, mutable and continuous.

The mutability is lost even in the kind of linguistic analysis which both appreciates and classifies detail. The two linguistic studies in this book move very slowly, dwelling long on particular words and phrases, and certainly do not lose the sense of particularity in a broad-meshed net. The structural critic may stride over particular effects to draw an outline-map of scenes, images, symbols and persons, but the analyst of language crawls faithfully over the page. Perhaps he crawls so slowly that the word 'faithfully' becomes a little imprecise. His snail's pace may strike us as necessary, like the camera called in to determine the photo-finish, but as too slow to give a full record of the impressions of responsive reading. Reading speeds vary, but the linguist's pace is plainly much slower than the pace of the slowest reader, just as the image-tracker's seven-league boots move him much faster than the fastest reader. The snail's pace keeps us close to the word, to its nuances, associations, typicality, and particularity, but it has to stop for a long scrutiny which regards each part while unnatural arrest takes place, while moments are attenuated or cut in sections, while the cellular structure is revealed and the surface removed. The analyst of language moves slowly, the analyst of total structure moves fast: one gives an exaggerated close-up, the other a long-shot. Both standardize and falsify, neglecting the completeness, movement, and complexity of reading experience. Both lose touch with the surface of the novel.

Such distortion is necessary. To object would be to object to the microscope or the telescope, to methods and machinery which reveal and discover. I wish only to say that we need to admit the distortion, and not to pretend—as we sometimes tend to do—that an analysis of syntax or typical vocabulary or imagery is a total analysis. I do not agree with Spitzer[1] that one can get at the heart of the work of art from many directions. Direction and method may well determine result. I do not want to claim that a close look at detail will tell us much about total structure, but only that it takes its place in the investigation of the nature of fiction, and especially of the novels of George Eliot. I would however, claim that an analysis of the surface should counteract the necessary distortions of linguistic and formal analysis, despite the restrictions of its discovery.

There are, no doubt, many ways of organizing a study of detail. We might proceed by taking one or two striking and symbolic images and then looking at their local and particular effect in relation to and in distinction from their function as epitome. We might choose some striking but apparently isolated images, and look at them in their local context. We might take the presentation of minor characters or minor events, or look at 'background' material like description of places, objects, or gestures. I decided to choose a chapter and look at the various details it contains. I chose Chapter 30 at random since any part will do to represent the continuous surface of the novel. It so happens that it is an interestingly mixed chapter, more relaxed and heterogeneous than, say, Chapter 28, which presents Dorothea's disenchanted awakening, or Chapter 80, which presents her vigil after she has seen Ladislaw with Rosamond, or Chapter 83, her last scene with Ladislaw. These are all scenes of crisis in action, but all also highly compressed and pregnant. Chapter 30 is also less blatantly and totally symbolic than other

154

scenes which do not mark such crises of decision, but are plainly summaries and potent expressions of idea and feeling, like the scene in Rome where Casaubon takes Dorothea on a tour of significant works of art, or the scene of Featherstone's funeral, or the scene where Mary Garth and Rosamond look together in the mirror. Chapter 30 does however mark a very important stage in the action: in it Dorothea is told that Casaubon's illness is fatal, and must change his way of life, and it ends with Brooke's decision to invite Ladislaw to Middlemarch. It is morally important, involving Dorothea's declaration of unselfish love and desire to help, her cry to Lydgate, and his warm but helpless response. It uses symbolism, but in a diffuse and unarresting way, as I shall try to show.

It is difficult to find a chapter in this novel which contains neither a crisis in action nor a crisis in vision. Although the texture is more dense and the epitomes less glaring than in the novels of Henry James, there is very little relaxation of tension in *Middlemarch*, very much less assertive comic play, casual filling-in and local colour than in the Victorian-Gothic structures of Dickens or Trollope. *Middlemarch* has its choric scenes of gossip and crowd-reaction presenting the character of the community, as in the scene of the auction, for instance, or the talk of the women at Mr Brooke's first dinner-party, but these passages are parts, not whole chapters, and usually share the chapter with more crucial and symbolic material. Nearly all the chapters have the same form of organization. There is a dominance of dialogue and action, and this is usually grouped into one, two, or three scenes, separated and steadily bridged by exposition or report. There is a frequent change of scene, of persons, place, and time, but within a fairly restricted framework. We move from one room to another but very often stay in the same house, or move from one part of the day to another but with the same people. Sometimes time is indefinite, faintly and usefully blurred. There are some chapters which have very little exposition, but there are none with no scenic material. Exposition overlaps with scene, for it is dotted with scenic images, and is often vividly and immediately sensational, while scene is seldom purely dramatic but uses commentary and description as well as dialogue. George Eliot's typical chapter, in *Middlemarch*, achieves a loose unity, often with a local concentration of ideas, atmosphere and symbol, as well as of time and place. She often uses her varied and modulated materials to push on time and action *during* rather than *between* chapters.

Chapter 30 begins with a very brief scene between Casaubon, Lydgate, and Brooke, at Lowick, which is followed by the long and central scene between Lydgate and Dorothea. This modulates into a report of Dorothea's thoughts and doings after Lydgate goes, and eventually, after a longer and rather indeterminate interval, presents Brooke writing the crucial letter asking Ladislaw to come to Middlemarch. The very beginning of the chapter moves us on from the point at which we left Casaubon at the end of Chapter 29, when he had his first heart attack. In Chapter 30 we are told how 'in a few days' Casaubon 'began to recover his usual condition'. Then there follows an uncommitted past tense in which Lydgate sits and watches by the sick man, obviously on more than one occasion. At last a particular occasion is singled out to make the first scene, in which Lydgate advises Casaubon 'to be satisfied with moderate work, and to seek variety of relaxation'. Next comes another vague past-continuous tense, going back beyond the scene to various times when Dorothea had been present 'by her husband's side'. Lydgate 'had determined on speaking to her' and when Brooke makes the suggestion as they stand 'outside the door' of Casaubon's sickroom, he decides to do it there and then, asks for her, is told that she is out, and waits until she comes in.

Then we reach the central scene, long, detailed, chronicling every word and movement and feeling, co-terminous with the whole experience and leaping over nothing. It deals very fully and faithfully with the present but has one or two moving flights into the past (Dorothea's 'if I had known') and into the future ('For years after Lydgate remembered'). Lydgate goes and time moves on slowly as Dorothea, still in the library, reads the letters on the writing-table and then ends by giving Ladislaw's letter to 'her uncle who was still in the house'. He writes the reply to Will at Lowick and apparently on the same day: we are told that 'he went away without telling Dorothea what he had put into the letter, for she was engaged with her husband, and —in fact, these things were of no importance to her'.

Time moves on, at first quickly, then very slowly indeed, foreshortening nothing. Elsewhere this forward progression covers much larger periods, as for instance in the next chapter, though here George Eliot uses the same device of picking up exactly where we left off in the previous chapter and making the leap within the chapter. In Chapter 31 we begin on the evening of the same day and we have Lydgate off duty with Rosamond, to whom he talks about the day's happenings—in particular about Dorothea's reactions and the strong impression they have made on him. In the following section we return to the indefinite past-continuous, 'Aunt Bulstrode, for example, came a little oftener', and thus we proceed a fair distance in time. My chosen chapter provides less exciting examples of this form of movement than others, including its successor and its predecessor, but it does reveal what I think is the typical pattern: overlap or coincidence of time, foreshortening by a past-continuous, movement within rather than between the chapters, and smooth transition. This kind of structure is one of the things revealed by a close look at detail.

George Eliot's central events, however, take place within a unity of time and place, and local unity is another important feature of her manipulation of time. In this chapter there is great compression, and in others there is more variety and movement. Here we have three or four conversations and events, all involving the same people, and taking place on the same day in the same house. George Eliot's timing presents not only a slow and detailed chronicle but a very natural, almost casual, flow. Events and dialogue appear to be connected by proximity, not by careful selection. The transitions themselves are often unexciting, undramatic, and inconspicuous, and the structure is superficially episodic, not appearing as prologue, main action, and epilogue, as it usually does in a Jamesian chapter. This episodic and almost casual appearance *is* only an *appearance*, since of course selection is taking place all the time. The structure is governed by the relations of proximity, the appearance suggests the loose unity of 'everything that happened at

Lowick on that day' but crisis is present at each stage. Casaubon is more or less told to give up his work. Dorothea is informed, and grasps the loss and desolation for him, and the awful helplessness involved for herself. The action leading up to Ladislaw's invitation, the beginning of another crisis, is all strictly necessary and plausible. The crises are all revealed and relaxed by the insensitivity of Brooke, whose suggestions of shuttlecock and Smollett and final almost automatic writing to Ladislaw are splendid instances of what Henry James called the fool's ministrations to the intensities of others. In the first scene Brooke lays bare the intensity he cannot grasp, in the last he shows himself as the only person sufficiently unaware to summon Ladislaw to Middlemarch. He is an ironically chosen maker of destinies. Action pushes ahead at each stage: most important, the reader looks ahead with the characters to the obscure future where Casaubon must relax, where Dorothea will try to help him. This is not just a matter of looking forward, since involved in the look is uncertainty and question: how can he possibly relax, how can she possibly help him? We are left too with the growing attachment of the book title, *Waiting for Death*, to Casaubon and Dorothea as well as to Featherstone.

The book title makes itself sharply felt in this and in the previous chapter, not simply in the subject of the grave illness but also in the emphasis on waiting in general. Looking at single chapters brings out this kind of local emphasis, which I should prefer not to call 'theme' or 'motif', since it scarcely reaches the level of generalization and is really not very conspicuous. However, it is there, and naturally enough. It plays its part in the feeling of the chapter, where watching and waiting are thoroughly explored through many aspects. We observe frustration, fear, anxiety, understanding, insensitivity, love, sympathy, and professional detachment blended with that good humane curiosity informed by imagination. It is not just the action of waiting with which many of the chapters in this book are concerned, but the feelings with which human beings may wait. Lydgate is the first to watch and wait, and we are carefully told that he does this in different ways: he uses the newly invented stethoscope but he also sits quietly by the patient and watches him. His quiet

158

watchful patience, and his conversation with Casaubon about being satisfied with moderate work, are among those details of professional character which make us feel that Lydgate is a good doctor, and that being a good doctor has something to do with being a good man. A little later we are told that he also watched Dorothea as she watched and waited:

She was usually by her husband's side, and the unaffected signs of intense anxiety in her face and voice about whatever touched his mind or health, made a drama which Lydgate was inclined to watch. He said to himself that he was only doing right in telling her the truth about her husband's future, but he certainly thought that it would be interesting to talk confidentially with her. A medical man likes to make psychological observations, and sometimes in the pursuit of such studies is too easily tempted into momentous prophecy which life and death easily set at nought. Lydgate had often been satirical on this gratuitous prediction, and he meant now to be guarded.

Unlike so many watchers in *Middlemarch* Lydgate is concerned to observe Dorothea, to learn about her, to make no predictions about her marriage, feelings, and future. His imaginative tact in this scene shows the delicacy and tenderness in his character (ironically neighbouring the spots of commonness) which are to emerge so significantly in the shaping of his and Rosamond's destinies. This delicacy is brought out more plainly in the following chapter when he tells Rosamond how moved he has been by Mrs Casaubon's strong feeling for a man thirty years her senior, and when Rosamond's brashly conventional and ignorant rejoinder makes another strand in the web of irony.

All the characters in Chapter 30 watch and wait. Casaubon has to wait, to try to 'relax', to pass time. Dorothea has to wait, feeling remorse, responsibility, and helpless love. She who has been a great collector of lame dogs, and has met the hardship of finding no lame dogs to nurse in Lowick, now finds herself faced by a great need and can do little. Here Dorothea finds a cause, but cannot battle. The only character who is not centrally involved in watching and waiting is Brooke, whose reactions frame the central scene, whose role here is his role elsewhere in the novel, that of the fool who rushes in but avoids all real commitment. His comments are benevolently maladroit. The ironies of his reference to toy-making (in this house and this family) and the 'it's a little broad, but she may read anything now she's married, you know', are embedded in his flow of well-meaning futile chatter. This barely touches the real conversation between Casaubon and Lydgate, who have little enough in common but are both serious men, here brought together by their understanding of professional seriousness and values. Brooke never actually comes into real communication with anyone in this chapter and his detachment shows at its beginning and at its end.

The decisive event which is comically and ironically framed by Brooke's detachment is Dorothea's reaction to Lydgate's bad news. The form of the chapter reflects in some ways the form of the novel. George Eliot has chosen to call this book, *Waiting for Death*, and to spend most of her imaginative energy showing the waiting done by Dorothea. Throughout the novel the significant departures from Dorothea's point of view—'Why always Dorothea?'—emphasize the normative function this performs. It is she, not Casaubon, who is central in the chapter and in the novel. There are withdrawals, opacities, and foreshortenings in the treatment of Casaubon, very few in the treatment of his wife.

Dorothea comes in to hear the tragic news, from her walk with Celia, radiant and glowing. The 'glow' has been established already, and represents her vitality and her physical youth and health. She comes in from the outside world of health and light, and these vital qualities recede as she goes into the library with Lydgate. What follows is the breaking of the news and a moral crisis. Dorothea does not consciously weigh and choose, as on some occasions before and after, but here spontaneously chooses love. She has stopped resenting, wanting, and criticizing, and she thinks of herself in relation to Casaubon only as a possible and frail source of help. She has broken with the past Dorothea who has usually spoken and acted from a sense of her own trials, has stopped listening to her own heartbeats and thinks only of the feeble ones of her husband.

If it is, in George Eliot's terms, an 'epoch' for her, so it is for Lydgate. There is yet another strand in the contrast between

Dorothea and Rosamond: 'Women like Dorothea had not yet entered into his tradition.' He makes no rash predictions, but waits with rare sensitive concern, then 'wonders' about her marriage. He is that unusually imaginative man who does not impose categories and who does not gossip. This is a novel where George Eliot is concerned to show how character fits (or does not fit) profession, and how profession shapes character. Lydgate is a fine example of the consistency and subtlety of her psychological and professional detail. Dorothea's spontaneous cry, 'Tell me what I can do?' is to be picked up on several later occasions but here it marks very sharply that naked contact of real feelings which makes a crisis in many different kinds of relationship in the novels of George Eliot.[2] Here Dorothea's helplessness meets Lydgate's helplessness, but the communication makes a living and lasting relation between them.

In action and in feeling, the chapter is crucial, and we see George Eliot underpinning it to past and future, not just in the references to time but also in its symbolic associations. We pick up tones of light and dark from past scenes where Dorothea has stood out from Lowick, from past scenes in the library. We hear tones which are to resound and accumulate in later contrasts between Dorothea and Rosamond, and later scenes where Dorothea's moral energy is seen to be linked with the 'epoch' here marked. If we consider this chapter as 'an organ to the whole' there is abundant material: the recurring antithesis of light and darkness, the particular forms of Lowick and the dim room, the small windows, and the world outside, all connect with many interwoven series of images and symbols in the novel. So too does the cry 'Tell me what I can do?', the significantly expressive use of clothes, and the image of a marble statue. I should like to take some of these familiar structural symbols and to bear in mind both their place in the pattern and their local impact in this chapter.

Only one of these images is made conspicuous by being generalized within the chapter. This is the contrast of darkness and light. I should add that it is also the image which has already been most fully developed before we meet it: in many small metaphors and in the elaborately expressive description of

Lowick in Chapter 9, and in Ladislaw's violent conspicuous extensions. What additional impressions are made in Chapter 30? The library is dark, because it has been left shuttered: 'But there was light enough to read by from the narrow upper panes of the windows'. The light which is let in is described by a tiny arbitrary reminder of its scholarly occupier, which also acts as preparation—if the room were too dark Dorothea would not be able to read Will's letter later on. But there is no immediate question of anyone wanting to read. The 'narrow' is also a detail which seems redundant in the immediate context, but makes a link with the associations already established in the early descriptions of 'small-windowed and melancholy-looking' Lowick. The first description of the library itself, ironically placed in the radiantly optimistic vision of Dorothea before her marriage, mentions 'dark book-shelves', 'curtains with colours subdued by time'. The small windows, birds-eye views on the walls, and Casaubon's revelation of his own 'sufficiently large' views of women, are contrasted with the bow-window of Dorothea's room, and make their small but unmistakable contribution to the details of visionary symbol. (Chapter 9 is full of imagery of views and darkness and light from which I have merely chosen a few examples.) We are told that Lowick is the kind of house 'that must have children, many flowers, open windows, and little vistas of bright things, to make it seem a joyous home', and we have also met Casaubon's lack of interest in houses for people to live in, and his preoccupation with narrow Egyptian dwellings, tombs and catacombs. The library itself is later to be dubbed 'a caticom' by Tantripp. It is obviously the centre of what Will Ladislaw calls the stone prison and the labyrinth, the room most darkened and subdued by Casaubon's sterile and isolated gloom. Will is of course associated with light and colour, Dorothea with open windows and outward gaze, and the symbolic antithesis of light and dark is to cover many implications of fertility and sterility, breadth and narrowness, life and death—in value and expression natural and common and not confined to this novel or this novelist. How do we read the images of darkness here?

I do not think that we read them primarily as symbols of

Casaubon, in spite of the details that attach them to the main pattern of value and feeling. For instance, when Dorothea says to Lydgate, 'You will not mind the sombre light', this is, I think, to be taken at its face-value, with some appropriate and immediate associations with Lydgate's habituation to the valley of the shadow of death. Death does, after all, hang over this book. Her words about the sombre light stand also for Dorothea's acceptance of gloom. But they are primarily an indication of Dorothea's trusting, genuine casualness and informality in dealing with Lydgate in this situation. We are told that Lydgate remembered for years after Dorothea's cry of appeal: 'this cry from soul to soul, without other consciousness than their moving with kindred natures in the same embroiled medium, the same troublous fitfully-illumined life'. Here the dark and the light are generalized and stand for the variegation of human life, and the darkness is that of suffering, death, obscurity, the light perhaps of hope, joy, lucidity. The antithesis acts like the image of the lighthouse in *To the Lighthouse* and does not belong to the Casaubon/Ladislaw or the Casaubon/Dorothea contrast. George Eliot has established a pattern to which she can refer briefly and reliably, as in the easy association in the previous chapter between Casaubon's mood and 'the foggy morning', but it is not a rigidly insistent pattern, and the primary impressions of light and dark in Chapter 30 are likely to be falsified if we are concerned only to pluck them out of context.

Another image which we have already met before is the image of a marble statue. When Lydgate tells Dorothea that Casaubon may live for years, with great care, but that 'it is one of those cases in which death is sometimes sudden', Dorothea's physical reactions and feelings are described in this way:

There was silence for a few moments, while Dorothea sat as if she had been turned to marble, though the life within her was so intense that her mind had never before swept in brief time over an equal range of scenes and motives.

The most famous of the images of marble lies ahead, in Farebrother's dictum, 'Character is not cut in marble', to which Dorothea makes the incisive reply, 'Then it can be rescued and healed'. But we have met it before, in many forms, in many actual casts and statues. There are the incomprehensible casts brought home by Brooke, 'Whose severe classical nudities . . . were painfully inexplicable, staring into the midst of her Puritanic conceptions', and the marbles of Rome, on the wedding-journey, where 'the long vistas of white forms whose marble eyes seemed to hold the monotonous light of an alien world' make on Dorothea an indelible impression. (Incidentally, the accuracy of 'marble eyes' is another instance of a symbol working through precisely realized sensation—'marble eyes' holding 'monotonous light' is a superb description.) In the Vatican, 'she walked with him through the stony avenue of inscriptions', and she passes on listlessly to the Museum, while he goes to the library. She stands in the hall, where Naumann and Will Ladislaw find her:

Where the reclining Ariadne, then called the Cleopatra, lies in the marble voluptuousness of her beauty, the drapery folding round her with a petal-like ease and tenderness. They were just in time to see another figure standing against a pedestal near the reclining marble: a breathing blooming girl, whose form, not shamed by the Ariadne, was clad in the Quakerish grey drapery. . . . (Ch. 19)

Naumann makes explicit what he sees as the antithesis:

'What do you think of that for a fine bit of antithesis?' said the German, searching in his friend's face for responding admiration. . . . 'There lies antique beauty, not corpse-like even in death, but arrested in the complete contentment of its sensuous perfection: and here lies beauty in its breathing life, with the consciousness of Christian centuries in its bosom.' (Ch. 19)

In each of these examples, and in Farebrother's metaphor too, marble is brought into contrast with life, not as a form of death but as something fixed, arrested, and unconscious. Look again at the metaphor of marble in Chapter 30, remembering that Rome and Naumann are mentioned in the chapter, so that resonance from the earlier scene might well be expected and effective:

There was silence for a few moments, while Dorothea sat as if she had been turned to marble, though the life within her was so intense that her mind had never before swept in brief time over an equal range of scenes and motives.

It is a purely local simile, though a few lines later we have a reminder of Dorothea's 'pallid immobility'. What are we to say about this image? The art/life antithesis is a very important subject in *Middlemarch*, not merely because it forms the ambience for the character and career of Ladislaw, but because George Eliot is discussing the nature of asceticism and the function of art, as belonging to the analysis of society, as continuing Arnold's exploration in *Culture and Anarchy*, as relevant to the problems of Dorothea's feelings and values. Many characters are defined and even tested by their response to art, and art itself is defined and even tested by its relevance and meaning for human beings of different kinds. If we were making an analysis of artistic images in the novel, we might well include the simile in Chapter 30, and observe that it belonged to the symbolism of aesthetic value. If, however, we look at it in its context, it adds absolutely nothing to that theme, except in automatic reminder, for what that is worth. What is vivid here in this image is the local expression of Dorothea's shocked stillness and pallor, contrasting with the racing pulse of thought and feeling within. It is an image which shows both the transformation of feeling and the contrast between outside appearance and inner passion. It is this local vividness that is primary, not the structural contribution to patterns of imagery and to dominant themes of life and art. The superficial impression is the most important one.

This is probably a fairly uncontroversial example. More difficult is the symbol of clothes in this chapter. Dorothea first comes in with Celia, 'both glowing from their struggle with the March wind'. When Lydgate speaks to Dorothea, as we have seen, she behaves quite spontaneously, and opens the library door, 'thinking of nothing at the moment but what he might have to say about Mr Casaubon'. She leaves her outdoor clothes on, but a little later takes off her bonnet and gloves. There is the comment that she throws off 'her bonnet and gloves, with an instinctive discarding of formality where a great question of destiny was concerned'. The informality extends also to her action of sitting down, and her 'Sit down' addressed to Lydgate.

Her actions and attitudes are typically informal and unselfcon-
scious, but here there is a particular pointing. This is not just
Dorothea's usual genuine disregard for social formality, but the
informality produced by the crisis, the simplicity and unaffected
impatience that are the understandable response. This is also
felt after Lydgate has broken the news about Casaubon's illness:
'Lydgate rose, and Dorothea mechanically rose at the same time,
unclasping her cloak and throwing it off as if it stifled her.'
Here we go beyond the unstudied impatience and spontaneity
of the earlier detail: this action of throwing off the cloak is also
expressive of violent feeling. In this chapter George Eliot uses
Dorothea's clothes not as symbols of value but as changing and
highly expressive properties. Clothes are certainly important
symbols in this novel, as associated with Dorothea, Celia,
Rosamond and Mrs Bulstrode, and in larger traditional ways
which draw on the aesthetic and social values with which history
has invested clothing, ways which perhaps owe something to
Swift and Carlyle. People's attitudes to their clothes symbolize
surface and appearance, vanity, exhibitionism, flaunting of sex,
of class, over-decorativeness, materialism, extravagance and so
on. There are local nuances: Dorothea does not 'deck' herself,
Celia and Rosamond do, Dorothea changes from deeper mourning
to light, Mrs Bulstrode takes off her ornaments.[3] It is attitudes to clothes, rather than the actual clothes, which are important. This scene in Chapter 30 is particularly interesting because
in it nothing at all is said about what the clothes are like. It is
what is done with them that matters. Dorothea's informal
throwing off her garments is in perfect keeping with her neglect
of appearances, conventions, propriety, and vanity. It is in
perfect keeping with her relationship with Lydgate. And it is
in perfect keeping with the grave crisis, when polite formality is
too slow and too fussy for deep feeling. Ceremony has broken
down. We grasp the expression of these values, but grasp also
that the actual gestures are expressive of strong feeling, of
impatience, urgency, desire to break out and breathe or do
something, need for relief, action, getting down to essentials—
this unwieldy list comprises many reactions we might lump
together under the reaction from frustration or tension. The last

casting off of the cloak is attached to the other gestures and movements in the chapter, and this again is part of the continuum we are likely to ignore and break up if we jump from image to image. Dorothea's attitude to her clothes belongs to the whole presentation of her person and personality and character in this place at this time.

She sets the tone with 'You will not mind this sombre light'. When she addresses Lydgate she is 'standing in the middle of the room' and she does not invite him to sit down for some little time. When she does, she speaks rather abruptly. She begs him to speak plainly, she reacts quickly, her words come out 'like a cry'. The word 'quick' is used of her 'ear' which detects significance in the doctor's tone of voice, and of her 'prevision' of Casaubon's wretchedness. Her voice is described in detail: it is imploring, like a cry, then low, then has 'a childlike despondency' while she actually cries, and her last appeal to Lydgate, 'Think what I can do' is made 'with a sob'. George Eliot is following the detail of voice and movement: we know what Dorothea sounded like, where she stood or sat, how she moved or stayed motionless. We know too how each sound and movement came from the last. The movement of feeling, so much more detailed here than in the framework which begins and ends the chapter, is composed of simple straightforward non-figurative description as well as of metaphors. The metaphor of the marble statue and the cry of 'soul to soul' are placed in a very precise and physical record of movement and speech, some of which is expressive, some apparently there to make a natural flow of acting and doing. People talk, take off their outdoor clothes, come in from walks, notice or do not notice their surroundings, sit down and stand up. Rooms have been changed or left alone since the last time we saw them. The continuum is natural, but it allows for climax. The ordinary actions stop when Dorothea makes her cry for sympathy, which comes quite naturally out of all that has gone before, but strikes the reader, like Lydgate, as a baring of feeling in a crisis presented in decorous and far from unusual terms: after all, people do keep doctors standing up while they put their questions, and do weep in their presence.

After Lydgate goes, the natural track of movement continues, variously and fluently. Although she is alone, she stops crying at the thought that she must keep her tears from Casaubon. She goes to the table, looks at the letters, and reacts to Will's outpoured 'young vivacity' by seeing that it is 'impossible to read' it at that time. The very lack of comment is masterly. Nothing is said about her feelings, she just sees what kind of letter it is and sees that it has nothing to do with the here-and-now. She passes on to give the other letter, addressed to Casaubon, to her uncle. Even the ironical introduction of 'her lack of sturdy neutral delight in things as they are', as Will sees it and puts it, meets the reader unemphatically, with no need for comment on the present crisis which has made everything different, and rendered their debate in Rome theoretic and very far away. It is a most beautiful showing of her control and her commitment, unemphatic and restrained in form as in content.

This central scene is composed of many incidents, tones, and narrative methods. The author's commentary, for instance, is often dramatically appropriate, as in the comments on Lydgate's watching or his withdrawal from rash prediction, or on Dorothea's marble appearance and passionate feeling, or on the process of Brooke's decision to ask Will to Middlemarch, made less by Brooke than by his pen: none of these comments, if we reflect, could have been dramatized or expressed directly through character. The author's voice here, as so often in the later novels, is broken up, and is used functionally, to present and punctuate the dramatic scene. It does not hold up movement but facilitates it, filling in the movement backward or forward in time, standing back and staying silent, condensing urgent feeling into an image, or making a nice stroke of *erlebte Rede*,[4] as in the very last sentence in which Brooke goes away without telling Dorothea what he had 'put into the letter' since 'she was engaged with her husband, and—in fact, these things were of no importance to her'. The many small steps which we take here are made up of some material we call 'dramatic' and some material we tend to call 'undramatic'. My contention is that once we see the continuity and movement, especially of feeling, these divisions seem inappropriate. Voice of author and of characters blend in a naturally moving sequence which gives even to a scene of crisis the appearance and motion of life. The flow attaches us to the parts rather than to the whole, and makes a whole of a stanzaic unit, of the chapter itself.

In this chapter, carefully organized into a fluent but intricate three-part unit, George Eliot has concentrated on crisis and feeling. This is how certain people react to dying, their own and other people's. The detached attitudes of Brooke and Lydgate are delicately observed, and a spectrum of feeling is organized, though Casaubon's unanalysed response makes a stubbornly opaque streak, here as elsewhere. It is one of George Eliot's beautiful movements of decorum, that she witholds the internal commentary of Casaubon, and makes his questions and frustrated comments represent feeling, while the reactions of Lydgate and Dorothea are made fully available to us. She is in a later chapter (42) to follow Casaubon to 'the dark river-brink' in one of the most moving, solemn, and pathetically accurate movements of feeling and reflection, but as yet he is literally the patient, not knowing the implications of Lydgate's watching, which he is later most courteously to praise for its 'scrupulous care', in a phrase which takes us back to this chapter of watching. Other scenes are more strikingly subtle and novel in their psychological analysis, for here George Eliot is relying on impressions already built up and consolidated, though we should notice the new stroke of Lydgate's relationship with Casaubon, forming over the obtuse chatter of Brooke, and that of Lydgate's developing relationship with Dorothea. Both strokes add to character, and are also very important in the creation of local feeling. A character created by George Eliot is made up not only of a carefully arranged sequence of moral choices but also of a variety of feelings. Those feelings are very important in our experience of characters as 'real'. They are not always arranged in the carefully sequential pattern of the moral crisis. For instance, once Lydgate has chosen to vote for Tyke rather than Farebrother, we recognize his susceptibility to the varied pressures of Middlemarch, and we can all eventually nod wisely when he makes a similar choice in the matter of Raffles's death. In this kind of regular development the characters in the novel are much more schematic and steady than real people. But perhaps we accept this kind of moral schematism because it is truthfully presented in the solid and directly expressive forms of feeling. It is not true that Lydgate's strong feeling for Dorothea in Chapter 30 changes anything he does: in the very next chapter we see the fatal ease with which he can absorb, or scarcely notice, Rosamond's prettily and dishonestly phrased words about Dorothea and Casaubon. But for the reader he is changed: we have felt, not just been told, that those spots of commonness are really spots in a very delicate and responsive substance, because we have felt his reactions to Casaubon and to Dorothea. This is the full response to character, and it should be made plain that it is a response to feeling which exists in its own right, as it does perhaps most lucidly and movingly in poems which do not give elaborate histories and causalities. In discussing plot and theme and character, we often overlook feeling, but in discussing local detail we stay close to the track of feeling.

When we encounter these characters subsequently, it is with the felt experience behind us. This seems to be important to the total life of the novel. If we compare the scenes of feeling involving Romola and Daniel Deronda, for instance, they will, I suggest, show themselves as lacking in this kind of continuous creation, where all characters respond and move fully, not only in major ways, plainly functional and purposive, but with the implication of total availability. The gestures and tones of Romola and Daniel are fewer and cruder, more intensively symbolic. There is a lack of the kind of detail I have mentioned here, which is so marvellously typical of *Middlemarch*. I cannot substantiate this kind of comparison in a short study nor can I substantiate what I have called the typicality of this kind of detail. As I said earlier, this is a crucial scene, and there are many scenes in the novel where the detail is looser and freer, in feeling, gesture, and sensuousness. This scene contains few objects, for instance. Some of the scenes in Dorothea's room, or in Mrs Garth's kitchen, or in the Lydgates' drawing-room, are filled with prolific examples of the detail which is neither totally symbolic nor painstakingly naturalistic, but which has a superficial vividness which plays a strong part in the life of the novel. The surface is not evenly transparent, the detail sometimes does and sometimes does not create an epitome. The surface is continuous, made up of a complex structure which our larger analysis can only touch on. The divisions in that continuity are many, and the units within book and chapter cannot be appreciated unless we look at them in a close and individual way. It is the detail of sense and feeling, the continuous flow, and the subtle organization within chapters, which I have tried to bring out in this examination of Chapter 30 as a specimen of the neglected surface of the novel.

8

A Plea for Ancient Lights

J. M. S. TOMPKINS

SINCE it has become orthodox to acknowledge George Eliot as the first modern English novelist, there has been a tendency to treat *Middlemarch* as a Sacred Book. The essential quality of such a document, until the time when its 'sacredness' becomes merely a historical label, is its applicability to the period of the reader, not in all its details, which inevitably bear the stamp of its origin, but in the truths it states and implies. There is a likeness, if it is not pushed too far, between the medieval handling of the Bible and the modern approach to *Middlemarch*. If the literal and even the historical meanings of the text appeared remote and irrelevant, the allegorical and the anagogical could be tried. In something the same way, story, character and setting—those prime data of the nineteenth-century novel—can be pushed aside with slight and sometimes imperfect inspection, while the keen analytic intellects of the modern critical scene apply themselves to elucidate the formal relations, the ideal structures, the metaphors, overt and submerged, and the key-words and phrases of the work in hand. Sometimes we are carried beyond the identification of conscious artistry and invited to discern, in sequences and recurrences of allied terms, the movements of the novelist's unconscious mind. Some of these words are no more than parts of the machinery of the language, reduced metaphors and dead symbols found in everyday talk, unrealized images with no salient meaning. But 'crumble' the text sufficiently, and there they are, and we may suppose that the unconscious is expressed through this subtle and archaic means; and since what is left of the doctrine of inspiration is now related to the activity of the unconscious, we may do well to study it *in minimis*, as early commentators studied the syllables of what they took to be the Holy Spirit.

172

It is not, therefore, with a myopic rejection of modern methods that I write this piece. They result naturally from the cultural pressures of our time, and the study of the novel can absorb all their findings. Moreover, the tendency towards abstraction, inherent in the sociological, structural, linguistic and even the psychological approach, is bound to encroach on the relish of the concrete and particular, as a book passes out of the hands of its contemporaries and the critic's line of sight gets longer. The delight of familiarity and recognition, which is a large part of contemporary reading, must fade. How soon it fades, particularly in a period of rapid social change, is brought home to anyone who reached maturity before 1914 and now meets the current generalizations about his period, class, notions and way of life. In a few years the fine gradations of veracity in a novel cease to be confirmed by observation, and the assumptions on which it could tacitly rest become matter of dispute and research. Where did comedy shade into caricature? At what point did a norm pass into an ideal type? The veracity of Dickens's London landladies was debated within a generation of his death, and Kipling's young officers and civilians are under discussion now. Immediate contact is lost; the living eye and ear no longer make their reports, and scholarship, which can answer so many curious questions, cannot reconstruct them; it can only inform the intellect. On the other hand, the larger divisions of human experience, the types, the generalized relations, the universal truths, are not so much subject to evanescence. The basic lines of the human landscape may show more clearly as its local and topical accidents lose their definition; and the critics, who by any process call attention to these, may be held to prepare the book for its immortality.

None the less, the modern student should not allow himself to overlook in a novel the 'hard particularities' (as Cleanth Brooks called them) of story, character, and setting. Their tints may be faded but their solidity remains. They are the author's overt statements, not to be ignored, and the best checks at our disposal on the findings of the schematic critics. For it would seem that their methods have no inbuilt checks. They are heady, and do not propose their own reasonable limits. These must be applied from outside by the common-sense and literary sensitiveness of the practitioner (imponderable qualities, not subject to statistics) and by continous reference to the text—not the shredded and crumbled text, from which almost anything can be extracted (as Swift pointed out in *A Tale of a Tub*), but the text in its original, coherent order, every image in its context, every word functioning primarily—whatever else it may do by the way—to drive on a story, establish a character, or define a conflict, a society or a scene. It is to this public daylight of the creative mind that I refer in the title of this paper. Windows that have illumined a dwelling-house for many years cannot lawfully be obstructed, but the indwellers may omit to look through them. It is only in their light, however, that we can detect where a vital metaphor or analogy declines into a conceit through elaboration of its accidentals, or where the prepossessions, which are the danger of the sociological critic, have effaced the precise lines of an individual situation. By their light, too, we can consider those parts of a book which fall outside or go beyond specialized interests, reminding ourselves that a novel is not only an artefact to be investigated but a world to be walked in, unless we would impoverish our responses. Lastly, in their light we may hope to correct those mistakes which we all make, in our several methods and periods, from prepossession, forgetfulness, and, even more, from the momentary blurring of the intently scrutinizing eye. Some of these are small and negligible, but some are disturbing and undermine confidence. Can we trust the location of a moral axis or the identification of thematic imagery by a critic who stumbles over the stated facts of the story?

A few examples must serve. One figure who seems to have eluded attention of late is Celia Brooke. Her structural function is simple and clear. She is the natural, almost unreflective conservative, happily placed in her surroundings, content with the opportunities they offer, keenly observant within the narrow circle of her interests, and disliking any 'notions' that criticize or disturb her world. In all this she is the opposite of her sister, as she is in her reserve and self-control; and the contrast is carried out in the different physical types of the girls and their ways of speaking. Celia's 'quiet' or 'comfortable staccato', her 'placid guttural' and 'neutral tone' evokes her personality even more strongly than Dorothea's rich and plaintive notes do hers. But there is much more to Celia than her functional values. There is her affection for Dodo, often apprehensive, disapproving and even resentful, and always miscomprehending Dorothea's passion for service (she calls the designs for agricultural dwellings that are, at first, its only outlet, Dorothea's 'hobby', and later distinguishes between the stopgap 'plans', which do no harm and keep her happy, and the alarming 'notions' that threaten subversive action) but still sisterly, abiding, and of a covered warmth. This affection is shown most strongly at the beginning and end of the novel, in the pallor and submissive change of manner with which she receives the news of Dorothea's betrothal, and in her only (and very timely) shower of tears, when she hears of her sister's dangerous childbed. But there are other gestures that express it, her removal of Dorothea's widow's cap on the hot summer's day and the 'touching distortion of her small features' when she drives to Lowick to remonstrate with her on marrying Ladislaw. The relations between the two are very thoroughly imagined. When we first meet her, Celia is a 'yoked creature' with 'private opinions'. The last outward sign of the yoke is the quakerish blue-grey pelisse, 'exactly like her sister's', in which she visits Dodo on her return from Rome. As sisters they have dressed alike, and the austere choice has been Dorothea's. Celia's opinions, whether private or expressed with 'a new sense of her mental solidity' as a young wife with a baby, are the occasion of some of George Eliot's most serene and genial passages. She is entirely at her ease with Celia, has no anxious explaining to do, and regards her creation with amused affection, particularly when she addresses herself to rational argument, as she does in the scene with the jewels. The language she uses is nicely differentiated from Dorothea's. Its habitual flatness and naïveté are never described as 'child-like'. They are partly the result of a literal mind, but even more of a sense of decorum that shrinks from the fully expressive as ridiculous. Her small range of tone includes the ruthless common sense with which she dismisses the dead Casaubon as 'spiteful', and tells Dodo that she should be grateful he has been taken away; but it is George Eliot as narrator who has to tell us that when Celia first suspected Dorothea's interest in Casaubon, she 'felt a sort of shame mingled with a sense of the ludicrous'. Celia would not so analyse herself; but her healthful instinct and young intolerance are some relief to the reader watching Dorothea's high-souled blunder. Celia, in short, is presented throughout the novel with a creative fulness of delicate and humorous detail and an effect of complete knowledge and spontaneity; and not much of it is relevant to the interests of the schematic critic.

Will Ladislaw is, however, relevant, since on what he is, at least potentially, must depend our judgment of the outcome of Dorothea's efforts. No-one has claimed Ladislaw as one of George Eliot's great successes, but this does not diminish his importance in the scheme of the book, though it must influence its total effect. He is presented in terms of youth—he and Dorothea are twice compared to two children—of bright intelligence and quick, mutable susceptibility. He has a rebellious temperament, the standards and manners of a gentleman, and a charm transmitted in images that are now somewhat faded—the tossed curls, the Cavalier portrait—but can still be seen to imply refinement, a proud impulsiveness and a capacity for ideal loyalty. His artist friend calls him 'dilettantish and amateurish', but the political work, to which he comes by chance, begins to exercise his full abilities. Yet he is not fully stable: when he believes he has lost Dorothea's trust, he dreads 'his own dislike for his spoiled life, which would leave him in motiveless levity'. It is Dorothea, whose love, as Lydgate discerned, 'might help a man more than her money', who gives him the stability to do the work that is in him.

It is of this character that Professor Mark Schorer writes: 'Given the metaphoric texture [of *Middlemarch*] one cannot escape the nearly systematic Christ analogy which George Eliot weaves around Ladislaw, omitting from her figure only the supremely important element of Christ's sacrifice, and the reason for which He made it.'[1] Meeting with this sentence out of its context, one might suspect that this is yet another case of analogy that has been elaborated into a conceit; that the cardinal Theresa-image has been prosecuted until the divine espousal of the nun has been equated with Dorothea's marriage, and Ladislaw with the bridegroom Christ. But this does not appear to have been the case. Professor Schorer, giving examples of 'the interpretive function of metaphor', picks out 'the clerical subject interpreted by the pseudo-religious theme: the true "religious" dedication of a Dorothea Brooke, and the characters around her falling into various "religious" postures: Casaubon as the false prophet, Bulstrode as the parody-prophet, Lydgate as the nearly true prophet—a "scientific Phoenix" he is called—somehow deflected from his prophecy; and Ladislaw as the true prophet.' Then follows the sentence quoted above. We can confine ourselves to Ladislaw and, carefully respecting the limits set on the analogy, ask first what attitudes and metaphors can be found in the text to support such a comparison and, secondly, whether on inspection they prove to be strong enough to weigh down its astonishing unlikelihood.

The attitudes and metaphors which may be held to support the Christ-image of Ladislaw seem to be the following:

(a) his association with light; the first impression on seeing him was one of 'sunny brightness'; his smile gushes like sunshine; his hair seemed to 'shake out light' (the Transfiguration?) and to Dorothea he seemed like a lunette window in her stony prison (the tomb?);

(b) his love of children (though this is described as 'half-artistic, half-affectionate');

(c) his sympathy; Dorothea thinks him 'likely to understand everything', 'a creature who entered into every one's feelings';

(d) the devotion he wakes in the quaint little old maid Henrietta Noble, who is ready to take his shoes for a pillow.

It is a suggestive list. It should, however, be noted that all these images, when they are found in the due course of the novel, are accompanied by the sense of the speaker (or thinker), and are liable to suffer some discount in consequence. We are aware that the starvation of Dorothea's sympathies in her marriage, and the obstruction of her ardent goodwill at all times, will lend a premature glory to any young Ladislaw. That is, some of the images are dramatic; they do not accumulate simply into a sum of mounting significance, but are shadowed by more or less clearly defined minus quantities. We may even have to discount George Eliot's own wistful pleasure in the physical beauty of the young. Moreover, these images occur in time, as we live through the novel, and they are interrupted and modified by quite different attitudes. There is, for instance, a set of recurrent descriptive adjectives and adverbs—pettish, wayward, petulantly, boyish, pouting, sulky, waspishly—which disturb the Christ-analogy considerably. In fact, what is successful in the portraiture of Ladislaw derives largely from the continuous accretion of discrepant suggestions about him, and the alertness with which we are incited to deal with them. If we take the last two paragraphs of Chapter 50 and the first of Chapter 51 we pass rapidly from Lydgate's description to Dorothea of Ladislaw 'gallanting' Miss Noble—'a sort of Daphnis in coat and waistcoat; and this little old maid reaching up to his arm'—to Dorothea's scornful rejection of Mrs Cadwallader's wounding parallel, 'an Italian with white mice', and her glowing evocation of him as 'a creature who entered into every one's feelings'. Then the next chapter opens with a Ladislaw busy with the election, irritable at Mr Brooke's cooling-off, and giving rather waspish answers to Lydgate. Each suggestion modifies all the others; nor can we really detach the metaphors from the actions that accompany them. Ladislaw is the man who can feel 'unspeakable content . . . that he was in the presence of a creature worthy to be perfectly loved' and can also undermine her respect for her husband's scholarship; he can fall into idle gallantry with Rosamond and turn on her with conscious cruelty when it exposes him to Dorothea; he can make a feast of gingerbread for ragged children and reject Bulstrode's expiatory generosity with fierce pride and no pity. His fluctuant qualities await the catalyst of Dorothea's love.

We can also take up the question by the other end and ask (still observing the required limitations) what are the salient characteristics of the Christ of the Gospels. A brief answer might point, first, to a deep certainty of his business in the world, the times and seasons connected with it, and its inescapable cost; and, secondly, to a magnetic charm. There is no need to dispute

Ladislaw's charm, and no way of making him conform to the first characteristic. George Eliot writes with benignant irony, when she introduces the graceful, indolent, young man, who disdains discipline, and holds that genius 'may confidently await those messages from the universe which summon it to its peculiar work, only placing itself in an attitude of receptivity to all sublime chances'. For this is no prose paraphrase of

Suffering, abstaining, quietly expecting,

whether in the carpenter's shop or the wilderness, and Ladislaw is no genius. He tells Dorothea: 'If things don't come easily to me I never get them.' In the end, that is not quite true, but he reaches his peculiar work by chance and lateral pressures. It is his anger at Casaubon's marriage that makes him reject his bounty, and his desire to stay near Dorothea that introduces him to political work. Lydgate, who has in this respect no bias, calls him 'a good fellow: rather miscellaneous and *bric-à-brac*, but likable.' By this *lumen siccum* the 'nearly systematic Christ analogy' looks like a cobweb.

It would extend this chapter too far to dilate on the other uses of ancient lights and, as regards mistakes, there is no need. There do not seem to be in *Middlemarch* criticism the same sort of factual errors as pursue, for instance, the heroes of Fielding. At most, one can point to a small area of foggy imprecision round the name Middlemarch. It makes a good title, memorable and lending itself to extended uses. It can stand for the whole cultural scene in the Midlands about 1830. It is this sense that Mr Quentin Anderson has in mind when he writes of *Middlemarch*: 'George Eliot has created a common medium which completely immerses most of her characters. It is hard to conceive how an individual can on this scene really originate anything. Dorothea's wide charity finds no direct expression; Lydgate's scientific interest in the town's health meets blank incomprehension and effectual resistance. . . . Indeed, the reader may by now feel . . . that Middlemarch is as oppressive as that provincial town inhabited by Emma Bovary.'[2] This is interesting as the reaction of a modern sensibility to the Midland scene. It is not quite, I think, George Eliot's reaction. For her there is always,

179

on one hand, some Caleb Garth, originating something in however small a way, and, on the other, some entrenched member of the older generation—Mrs Farebrother—to indicate that, however slowly, times do change. Even at its most oppressive, the book draws in fresh air through these small lungs. What Mr Anderson says of Lydgate is true, whether we take the name typically or locally, but this is not the case with Dorothea. Locally and socially, Dorothea does not belong to Middlemarch, and is not immersed in its atmosphere. Dorothea is county. Both before and after her marriage she lives in country houses several miles outside the town, which is her shopping town and the source of professional attendance. Her uncle dines prominent Middlemarchers when he intends to contest the seat, but the wives and daughters of the manufacturers are not invited. Sir James Chettam entertains Ladislaw, as Casaubon's cousin, but is troubled by the anomaly when he accepts a post on the Middlemarch press. Dorothea herself does not 'visit' in Middlemarch, and would hardly have done so, after her mourning was over, except as a patroness. To remember this is to give full value to the unimpeded spontaneity of her compassion in proposing to visit Rosamond. Nor is it true, in the local sense, to say that Middlemarch has obstructed her charity. She does not think of it as a possible field, until Lydgate tells her of the needs of the new hospital and, later, Bulstrode asks her to take his place as patron. Her maiden efforts are at Tipton and (through Sir James) Freshitt; the land she thinks of buying for her colony is in Yorkshire. It is true that her double hope of finding a proper channel for her money in the hospital and, at the same time, restoring Lydgate's purpose and standing, is disappointed when Lydgate, under pressure from many aspects of 'Middlemarch', withdraws from the town; but, had she been an older and a much colder woman, she could have kept on with the hospital and, with patient diplomacy, good advice and the support of her uncle and brother-in-law, confirmed it in the cause of medical reform. Such a woman could have fulfilled Sir James's vision of noble widowhood; but this was not a role for Dorothea. No doubt, disappointment—Sir James's advice against buying the Yorkshire land and Lydgate's refusal to continue the battle—

prepare her to accept defeat—if that is what we are to call it—but the most powerful agency in this defeat is not Middlemarch but Will Ladislaw and her own natural passion.

It remains to point out one inevitable consequence of schematic criticism; that is, the obscuring of the natural contours of the work in hand. A fine analysis of structure, a suggestive ordering of metaphoric material can provide enlightenment or challenge, but they flatten the living landscape of the novel into a diagram, where one line or node is as good as another to complete the pattern, and each recurrence of an image, whatever the occasion or mode, salient or trifling, emphatic or the merest convention —counts in the sum. To restore reality to the scene, to delineate the quality of the author, we require the ancient lights. George Eliot's intellectual power, imaginative sympathies and enormous pains raise every portion of her work as near to the same high standard of accomplishment as is possible in a novel of such a compass. Yet below all the conscious art and above (one supposes) all the subliminal activity, there remains a character, with definable traits, stronger in some things than in others, and consequently weaker in some things than in others. The writer who achieved those brilliant sequences in which Bulstrode negotiates with his God, and the austere and moving scenes with his wife, after his exposure, could not give body to such minor figures as Rigg and Raffles. She provides all we ought to need, including an ambition for Rigg, to stand in structural relation with the ambitions of Lydgate, Fred Vincy and Bulstrode; she helps herself with grotesque, but not improbably grotesque appearances, and batrachian and simian analogies, and works hard to get authenticity into their speech. Yet all remains flat and laborious, demonstrably true to fact but not at all lively, and we know that Trollope could have thrown off a sufficient sketch of these fellows as easily and rightly as George Eliot, on her own ground, finds the words and the half-conscious symbol with which Mrs Plymdale defends her friend Harriet Bulstrode in her calamity: 'She wears very neat patterns always. . . . And that feather I know she got dyed a pale lavender on purpose to be consistent. I must say it of Harriet that she wishes to do right.' (Ch. 74).

These characteristic and lively inequalities are also found in her satire. It is informative to list all the objects and states that sharpen her tongue, but classification cannot show us how much less good and wise she is in pure satire than in a mixed mode, when depreciation is mingled with some measure of humour, tolerance, benignity, even a sort of respect for the limited nature getting through the business of life with some decency. She has not the savagery of the pure satirist; she is never savage with Bulstrode; she feels the responsibility of truth too deeply. She imports Borthrop Trumbull, whom she regards with much geniality, into the eyrie of predatory passions at Stone Court. Without some loading of natural warmth, her briefer satirical observations are apt to become irritable scoffing, though they all carry their ballast of psychological observation. One of these acid sentences suggests that Dr Sprague was the more trusted for having no religion, 'the world-old association of cleverness with the evil principle being still potent in the minds even of lady-patients who had the strictest ideas of frilling and sentiment'. There is a similar coupling of incommensurables and a similar reduction of religion when she notes 'Mrs Bulstrode's naïve ways of conciliating piety and worldliness . . . a consciousness at once of filthy rags and the best damask', but this is softened by the word 'naïve'. Embroidered collars and Tuscan bonnets accompany this 'honest ostentatious' woman through the book, and we like her more and more. In the end we admire her, and think with kindness of her friendship with Mrs Plymdale, based on 'nearly the same preferences in silks, patterns for under-clothing, china-ware and clergymen' (the three-to-one propor-tion reflects her natural worldliness and her acquired religion) until, with Mrs Plymdale's defence about the lavender feather, the satire melts away.

There is a similar mixture of elements to be found in her erudite wit. Unmixed with sympathetic elements, it can decline to a pedantic archness. We see the classical allusion, of which she makes such learned and pungent use, at its best when it is mixed with common human material. Thus, while Rosamond sings at the piano to Lydgate, 'her mother sat, like a Niobe before her troubles, with her youngest little girl in her lap, softly beating the child's hand up and down in time to the music'.

It is in such mental habits and craftsman's devices as these, in their particular contexts and unfolding order, that the character of a writer is to be found.

NOTES

1. THE STRUCTURE OF THE NOVEL

1 Cf. pp. 59–61, 133–4 below.

2 I apologize for drawing on material that I have already published, but it seems so much to the point of what I regard as the problem here—mind and ideas— that I must summarize at least what I have said before in an essay called 'Fiction and the "Matrix of Analogy"', *Kenyon Review*, 11 (Autumn 1949).

2. THE INTELLECTUAL BACKGROUND OF THE NOVEL

1 Paris, 1933.

2 U. C. Knoepflmacher, *Religious Humanism and the Victorian Novel* (Princeton, 1965); B. J. Paris, *Experiments in Life; George Eliot's Quest for Values* (Detroit, 1965).

3 The point, briefly, is that George Eliot is delineating in Lydgate the emergence of a new kind of doctor, with new status and new ideas of medical practice. Consequently he arouses the jealousy of his more traditional colleagues. For a fuller consideration of this aspect of Lydgate see my edition of *Middlemarch* (Penguin Books, 1965).

4 'Early Grecian History and Legend', *Edinburgh Review*, October 1846. Collected in the second volume of *Discussions and Dissertations*, the whole essay is a striking, if oblique, commentary on many aspects of Victorian religious thought.

5 One by-product of this was the attempt to treat the Bible as literature. A pioneer in this field was Robert Lowth in his *De sacra poesi Hebraeorum* (1753). Casaubon asks Dorothea to read him some pages of Lowth in Chapter 37.

6 'Writing to Julius Hare in 1835—the year of the publication of Strauss's *Das Leben Jesu*—Thomas Arnold notes as one of the objects of a proposed theological review: "To make some beginnings of Biblical Criticism, which, as far as relates to the Old Testament, is in England almost nonexistent."' W. O. Raymond, *The Infinite Moment* (Toronto, 1965), pp. 20–1.

7 The fullest treatment of mythography is E. B. Hungerford's *Shores of Darkness* (New York, 1941). Much relevant material is also contained in E. Neff's *The Poetry of History* (New York, 1947). I am deeply indebted to both these books.

8 On the general background of biological thought *see* C. J. Singer's *A History of Biology* (London, 1959).

9 Henry James, review of *Middlemarch* in *The Galaxy* (March 1873); reprinted in *The House of Fiction* ed. L. Edel (London, 1957).

3. THE TEXT OF THE NOVEL

1 'George Eliot', *Blackwood's Edinburgh Magazine*, cxxix (February, 1881), p. 267. The article was apparently written by William Blackwood. See my *'Middlemarch' from Notebook to Novel* (Urbana, 1960), pp. 160–1.

2 Bound copies of the corrected proof of both these editions have been preserved by the publisher, William Blackwood and Sons. Wing Commander George Douglas Blackwood generously permitted me to consult them. Several sections of corrected proof of the first edition are missing: the 'Prelude'; much of

Ch. 16; Chs. 19–22; four pages near the beginning of Ch. 26; all of Book IV; Ch. 81 to the end of the novel including the 'Finale'. From the evidence of the extant corrected proof, it seems reasonable to conclude that relatively few of the differences between the manuscript and first edition are printer's or publisher's changes or errors.

3 The changes of these names in proof were necessitated by oversight, other appearances of these same names having been revised in manuscript (see Beaty, pp. 12ff.).

4 The switch was effected in order to keep Dorothea's story before the reader of the then bimonthly parts; the original sequence in which the Rome chapters opened Book III would have kept her 'off-stage' for four months. See Beaty, pp. 52–5. This switch is also evident in George Eliot's notebook—see Anna Theresa Kitchel, *George Eliot's Quarry for 'Middlemarch'* (Berkeley and Los Angeles, 1950), p. 47—and in the MS of the novel. As indicated in n.2, corrected proof of Chs. 19–22 of the first edition is missing; there are two proof versions of Chs. 23–6 (except for four missing pages near the beginning of Ch. 26), one of which reflects the earlier sequence. The splitting of what had been one chapter into present Chs. 20 and 21 required renumbering of all the later chapters in the part, but even in proof this had not been done, Book III ending with Ch. 32 instead of 33. The correction was made before the first edition appeared, however, presumably by printer or publisher.

5 Both involve the change of 'do not' to 'don't', once spoken by Dorothea (Ch. 5), once by Mary (Ch. 25).

6 Mr Vincy says 'them' in the first edition and "em' in MS on one occasion (Ch. 35), though there is no corrected proof of this section to confirm George Eliot's authority for the change.

Chapter 56, which contains both the Garth revisions noted here and two of the four spelled out contractions relating to him, as well as five of the seven relating to Fred, is the chapter in which Caleb is accosted by workmen while surveying for the railway, and Fred, coming to his aid, makes his choice of profession.

7 As may well be imagined, such Englishings are most common in *Romola*. Many more Italian words and phrases appear in the manuscript of that novel than in the *Cornhill* serial or first book edition. And the conversion continues; later editions of that novel, after the copyright reverted to the author and was sold to Blackwood, are virtually translations of the earlier editions.

8 The epigraph to Ch. 51 is, in manuscript, attributed to the mythical '*Mephisto in Britain*', the title deleted in proof. The source of the epigraph to Ch. 77 is, in manuscript and first edition, identified as *Henry VI P.I* but the printer correctly sets *Henry V* in proof of the 1874 edition (and makes two minor corrections in the epigraph itself), a note on proof, presumably GE's, saying 'your changes O.K.' In the same edition an allusion to Cyrus in the last paragraph of the novel is corrected from the earlier 'Alexander', as Haight indicates, p. 613.

9 'Tucker', now the name of Casaubon's curate, keeps cropping up in the MS attached to various characters, including Casaubon himself, before being discarded.

10 This kind of unconscious double entendre, which finds its way into the novels of the Brontës, for example, is usually caught in re-reading the manuscript or reading proof by George Eliot, or Lewes. A similar example appears in the MS of *Romola* (in print 'his poniard' replaces the phrase here italicized):

Baldassarre was not asleep. There was a square opening high in the wall of the hovel, through which the moonbeams sent in a stream of pale light; and if Tito could have looked through the opening, he would have seen his father seated on the straw, with something that shone like a white star in his hand. Baldassarre was feeling the edge of *that white thing*, taking refuge in that sensation from a hopeless blank of thought that seemed to lie like a great gulf between his passion and its aim. (Ch. 34)

11 Here and throughout this essay deletions will be indicated by italics.

In 1874 what had in MS and first edition been 'evangelicism' was set in type as 'religious doctrine' (Ch. 16), and, though there is no evidence that the change originated with George Eliot, she let it stand.

12 '. . . he was no radical in relation to anything but medical reform and the prosecution of discovery. In the rest of practical life he walked by hereditary habit; half from that personal pride and unreflecting egoism which I have already called commonness, and half from that *naïveté* which belonged to preoccupation with favourite ideas.' (Ch. 36)

13 This and the two preceding passages appear in Ch. 36, for which corrected proof of the first edition is missing. Proof changes have been inferred from comparing the MS and the first edition.

14 Here and throughout the essay the earlier version appears on the left.

In the last line 'Tertius' was substituted for 'Lydgate' in proof but deleted in favour of the original 'Lydgate'.

15 There are several revisions in proof within the added paragraph: 'most uncomfortable chill' was first 'terrible chill'; 'listening to' was 'hearing'; and the final sentence began, 'But when . . .'.

16 *The Novels of George Eliot* (London, 1959), pp. 189–200.

17 Though there is no further change in the 1874 proof, this and the preceding sentence are reduced to clauses introduced by colons. So, too, the Cabinet Edition. This apparent printer's change of punctuation somewhat de-emphasizes the staccato rhythm.

18 Earlier in this paragraph there are several minor adjustments, largely involving 'again' phrases. The phrase beginning the paragraph, 'He was again', was changed to 'Once more he saw himself', perhaps to compensate for the addition of two more clauses, involving hearing and feeling, which add 'again': 'Again he heard himself' (in the first edition, 'He heard himself again') and 'Again he felt himself'.

In the next two paragraphs there are a number of proof revisions, chiefly of temporal transitions: 'When came' to 'Then came'; '. . . congregation and became' to '. . . congregation. Soon he became'; 'For soon' to 'By-and-by'; 'Bulstrode was aware' to 'Bulstrode became aware'. The first two sentences of the first paragraph were originally questions: 'When came the moment of transition? Was it . . . richest man in the congregation and became . . . west-end trade?'

19 The contradiction between his doctrine and his actual 'religion of personal fear' is made a bit less pronounced by the deletion of an introductory phrase: '*For in spite of doctrinal refinements the kernel of* his belief in these moments of dread was, that if he spontaneously did something right, God would save him from the consequences of his wrong-doing.' This was to have been further de-emphasized by the deletion in proof of the next sentence—'For religion can only change when the emotions which fill it are changed; and the religion of personal fear remains nearly at the level of the savage'—but after deletion it is marked '*stet.*' in the proof.

20 Cf. p. 18 above, pp. 133–4 below.

4. THE LANGUAGE OF THE NOVEL:
THE CHARACTER OF DOROTHEA

1 W. C. Brownell, *Victorian Prose Masters* (1902), pp. 120–2.
2 Ibid. p. 145.
3 *The George Eliot Letters*, iii, 397.
4 *The Handling of Words* (1923), p. 61.
5 *Reading a Novel* (1949), p. 47.
6 *Early Victorian Novelists* (1934), p. 319.
7 *George Eliot Letters*, ii, 207.
8 *George Eliot Letters*, iv, 81. My italics.
9 The phrase she uses in her moving tribute to John Ruskin's *Modern Painters* iii: her review printed in *Westminster Gazette*, lxv (April 1856), p. 626.
10 *George Eliot Letters*, ii, 361–2.
11 *George Eliot Letters*, iii, 118.
12 *George Eliot Letters*, ii, 217.
13 Ibid., p. 246.
14 Ibid., p. 248
15 Ibid., p. 274.
16 *George Eliot Letters*, iii, 427.
17 Ibid., p. 374. 'Even in English this daring is far from being general. The writers who dare to be thoroughly familiar are Shakespeare, Fielding, Scott (where he is expressing the popular life with which he is familiar), and indeed any other writer of fiction of the first class. Even in his loftiest tragedies—in *Hamlet* for example, Shakespeare is intensely colloquial. *One hears the very accent of living men.*' (My italics.)
18 *George Eliot Letters*, ii, 362.
19 Cf. Luis Bunuel's film *Viridiana* (1961) for the study of a similar delusion.
20 Feuerbach, whose *Wesen des Christentums* George Eliot translated, distinguishes 'essential nature' from 'individuality'. *Essence of Christianity* (London, 1853), pp. 2, 275.
21 Randolph Quirk, *Charles Dickens*, University of Durham (1959), p. 23.
22 C. Bally, 'Le style indirect libre en français moderne', *Germanisch-Romanische Monatschrift*, iv (1912).
23 Lisa Glauser, *Schweizer anglistische Arbeiten* (Berne, 1948), pp. 118–19. 'Sie geht gründlich, tiefernst und gewissenhaft vor und analysiert mit einer leidenschaftlichen Wahrheitsliebe, die an die Brontës gemahnt, wahre und geheuchelte Motive. Ihre Menschen sind von innen gesehen und ihre Romane, äusserlich wenig handlungsreich, sind spannungsgeladene Dramen moralischer Konflikte . . . So ist hier also beides vereinigt: intuitive Innenschau und kritische Analyse; . . . und wir dürfen erwarten, [erlebte Rede] in reichem Masse und an zentraler Stelle verwendet zu finden.'
24 S. Ullman, *Style in the French Novel* (Cambridge, 1957), p. 104.
25 Ibid., p. 118.
26 Loc. cit.
27 Glauser, op. cit., p. 117. 'Nun war das Interesse für seelisches Erleben geweckt, . . . aber es fehlte das Gegengewicht, die Distanz, die Dämpfung, welche die andere Voraussetzung von [erlebte Rede] ist . . . In den Romanen der George Eliot nun finden wir zum erstenmal alle Bedingungen erfüllt, die die allseitige Ausbildung von [erlebte Rede] ermöglichen und sie zu dem ganz modernen Ausdrucksmittel werden lassen, als das wir sie kennen.'

28 Cf. E. H. Gombrich's brilliant discussion of style in the visual arts in *Art and Illusion* (1960), Part One.

29 *Linguistics and Literary History* (New York, 1962), pp. 18, 19.

30 Ibid.

31 John Ruskin, *Sesame and Lilies* (1871), p. 32.

32 Michael Riffaterre, 'Criteria for Style Analysis', *Word* (1959), p. 158.

5. THE LANGUAGE OF THE NOVEL: IMAGERY

1 Subsequently published as *Wise, Witty, and Tender Sayings of George Eliot* in December 1871 with a second edition in 1872 which included 'sayings' from *Middlemarch*. See *The George Eliot Letters*, i, lxxiv.

2 *George Eliot Letters*, v, 206.

3 G. H. Lewes, *The Life and Works of Goethe*, 2 vols. (London, 1855), ii, 13.

4 *Essays of George Eliot*, ed. Thomas Pinney (New York and London, 1963), pp. 17–18.

5 *George Eliot Letters*, v, 168.

6 '*Middlemarch*' *from Notebook to Novel. A Study of George Eliot's Creative Method* (Urbana, 1960), p. 123.

7 Of Dorothea's more immediate preoccupation at this time we are given a quite precise account. She was painfully aware of the need to let Celia know 'of the momentous change in Mr Casaubon's position since he had last been in the house'.

8 *Academy*, iv (1 January 1873), p. 3.

9 It is interesting to compare this image with that used by Virginia Woolf in *To the Lighthouse*: 'Here, she felt, putting the spoon down, was the still space that lies about the heart of things, where one could move or rest; could wait now (they were all helped) listening; could then, like a hawk which lapses suddenly from its high station, flaunt and sink on laughter easily, resting her whole weight upon what at the other end of the table her husband was saying . . .' (I. 17).

10 G. Wilson Knight, *The Wheel of Fire: Interpretations of Shakespearean Tragedy* (1949), p. 3.

11 The MS reads: *the* [which has perhaps been deleted] *detail . . . were.*

12 *Westminster Review*, lviii (October 1852), 435–59.

13 *George Eliot Letters*, i, lxxv.

14 'Philosophy of Style', p. 458.

15 'Worldliness and Other-Worldliness: The Poet Young', *Westminster Review*, lviii (January 1857), p. 30; *Essays*, ed. Pinney, p. 371.

16 Spencer, op. cit., p. 457.

17 'The Natural History of German Life', *Westminster Review*, lvi (July 1856), p. 54; *Essays*, ed. Pinney, p. 271.

18 'If [Mr Kingsley] would confine himself to his true sphere, he might be a teacher in the sense in which every great artist is a teacher—namely, by giving us his higher sensibility as a medium, a delicate acoustic or optical instrument, bringing home to our coarser senses what would otherwise be unperceived by us.' *Westminster Review*, liv (July 1855), p. 289: *Essays*, ed. Pinney, p. 126.

19 G. H. Lewes, *The Study of Psychology* (1879), p. 39.

20 *Essays*, ed. Pinney. p. 445.

21 12 February 1875. *George Eliot Letters*, vi, 125.

22 20 June 1871. Ibid., v, 155.

23 4 November 1872. Ibid., v, 324.
24 11 February 1873. Ibid., v, 374.
25 11 February 1873. Ibid., v, 373.
26 *Essays*, ed. Pinney, p. 145.
27 J. W. Cross, *George Eliot's Life as Related in her Letters and Journals*, 3 vols. (1885), i, 33.
28 Cross, op. cit., i, 36–7.
29 *George Eliot Letters*, i, lxvii.
30 [October? 1872]. *George Eliot Letters*, v, 322.
31. Ibid., v, 197.
32 15 July 1871. Ibid., v, 165.
33. 4 March 1872. Ibid., v, 252.
34 Cross, op. cit., i, 16.
35 15 November 1869. *George Eliot Letters*, v, 67.
36 Ibid., v, 177.
37 6 November 1869. Ibid., v, 65.
38 15 November 1869. Ibid., v, 67.
39 4 October 1869. Ibid., v, 57.
40 Ibid., v, 246.
41 2 vols. (Edinburgh and London, 1860), ii, 65.
42 Ibid., ii, 347–8.
43 *Life and Works of Goethe*, i, 291.
44 Ibid., i, 281.
45 4 December 1849. *George Eliot Letters*, i, 321.
46 B. de Spinoza, *Ethics*, part iii, prop. ii. Passages from George Eliot's ms translation of the *Ethics* are published here with the kind permission of the Librarian of Yale University.
47 Spinoza, *Ethics*, part v, prop. xl. dem. 'The more perfect a thing is, the more reality it has (by def. 6. part 2.) and consequently (by prop. iii. part 3 with its scholium) the more it acts and the less it suffers; and this demonstration proceeds in the same way in an inverse order. Therefore, a being is the more perfect, the more it acts; q.e.d.'
48 *George Eliot Letters*, ii, 211.
49 'Spinoza', *Westminster Review*, lxiv (July 1855), p. 29.
50 Spinoza's *Ethics*, part iii. dem.
51 'Spinoza's Life and Works', *Westminster Review*, xxxix (May 1843), p. 400.
52 Spinoza's *Ethics*, part ii, def. iii, 3.
53 *Westminster Review*, xxxix (May 1843), p. 399.
54 *Life and Works of Goethe*, i, 275.
55 *Westminster Review*, xxxix (May 1843), pp. 398–9.
56 *Essays*, ed. Pinney, p. 451.

6. CRITICISM OF THE NOVEL

1 The following essays and reviews are referred to in the text:
   The Academy, 1 Jan. 1873, pp. 1–4. (Edith Simcox.)
   The Athenaeum, 2 Dec. 1871, pp. 713–14; 3 Feb. 1872, pp. 137–8; 30 March 1872, p. 393; 1 June 1871, p. 481; 27 July 1872, p. 122; 7 Dec. 1872, pp. 725–6.
   The Atlantic Monthly, xxxi (1873), pp. 490–4.
   Blackwood's Edinburgh Magazine, cxii (1872), pp. 727–45. (W. L. Collins.)

The British Quarterly Review, lvii (1873), pp. 407–29. (R. H. Hutton.)

The Contemporary Review, xx (1872), pp. 403–22; xxix (1877), pp. 348–69. (Both by Edward Dowden.)

The Edinburgh Review, cxxxvii (1873), pp. 240–63. (Lord Houghton.)

The Examiner, 2 Dec. 1871, pp. 1192–3; 3 Feb. 1872, pp. 125–6; 30 March 1872; pp. 333–4; 8 June 1872, pp. 575–6; 27 July 1872, pp. 743–4; 5 Oct. 1872, pp. 985–6; 7 Dec. 1872, pp. 1204–5.

The Fortnightly Review, xiii (1873), pp. 143–4. (Sidney Colvin.)

The Galaxy, xv (1873), pp. 424–8. (Henry James.)

The London Quarterly Review, xl (1873), pp. 99–110.

The North American Review, cxvi (1873), pp. 432–40. (T. S. Parry?)

The Quarterly Review, cxxxiv (1873), pp. 336–69. (R. Laing.)

St Paul's Magazine, xii (1873), pp. 592–616. (G. B. Smith.)

The Saturday Review, 7 Dec. 1872, 733–4; 21 Dec. 1872, pp. 794–6.

The Spectator, 16 Dec. 1871, pp. 1528–9; 3 Feb. 1872, pp. 147–8; 30 March 1872, pp. 404–6; 7 Dec. 1872, pp. 1554–5. 'George Eliot's Moral Anatomy'; 5 Oct. 1872, pp. 1262–4.

The Times, 7 March 1873, pp. 3–4. (F. N. Broome.)

2 Cf. G. H. Lewes to John Blackwood (7 Sept. 1871): 'We have added on to the end of part I that portion of part II which closes with the scene at the miserly uncle's—a capital bit to end with; and this new arrangement not only pitches the interest forward into part II and prepares the way for the people and for Dodd's absence from part II, but also equalizes quantities better.' (*George Eliot Letters*, v, 184).

3 Cf. pp. 18, 59–61 above.

4 I suppose this could be said to be the main 'bias' in the contemporary reviews. Totally objective criticism is, of course, impossible; all critics are deflected from this theoretical absolute by some bias or other. For example, Henry James is an interested party because of his own creative concerns, Edith Simcox because of her passionate friendship for George Eliot. Other critics, as I have noted in my analysis of the *London Quarterly Review*, are deflected by the policy of their journal and the expectations of their readers. An almost comic example of this is the struggle of the *Quarterly* reviewer to do justice to *Middlemarch* in the face of his journal's conservatism and its dislike for the 'progressive', 'French' spirit which he detects in George Eliot's work. But the important thing is that he *does* struggle. The most any critic can do is to be aware of his own bias and to make allowances for it; in this most of the contemporary reviewers succeeded.

7. THE SURFACE OF THE NOVEL

1 *Linguistics and Literary History* (New York, 1962), p. 18.

2 See my *The Novels of George Eliot* (1959), pp. 104–5.

3 Cf. *The Novels of George Eliot*, p. 104.

4 Cf. Derek Oldfield's discussion of this technique, pp. 81–4 above.

8. A PLEA FOR ANCIENT LIGHTS

1 'Fiction and the "Matrix of Analogy" ', *Kenyon Review*, 11 (Autumn 1949).

2 From *From Dickens to Hardy*, ed. Boris Ford (Penguin Books, 1958).

INDEX

Note. This index is restricted to literary authors referred to by name or title, with the exception of the identifiable authors of essays and reviews discussed in Chapter 6. It may be noted that references to named persons excluded by this principle are largely concentrated in Chapter 2.